BREAD and BUTTER BOMBER BOYS

The Crew

BREAD and BUTTER
BOMBER
BOYS

Arthur White

A Square One Publication

First published in 1995 by
Square One Publications
The Tudor House,
16 Church Street
Upton on Severn, Worcs WR8 0HT

© Arthur White 1995

British Library Cataloguing in Publication Data
is available for this book

ISBN 1 872017 95 9

Typeset by Avon Dataset, Bidford on Avon
Printed by Antony Rowe Ltd, Chippenham, Wilts

To Paddy and Ian

Contents

FOREWORD By: Air Vice-Marshal W.J. Herrington, CB,RAF (Retd.)

List of Illustrations

Foreword

BY: Air Vice Marshal John Herrington C.B., R.A.F.(Retd.)

This is the story of one man and one crew from one squadron of Bomber Command which participated in the bomber offensive against Hitler's Reich and in support of the Allied ground offensive in Western Europe from September 1944 until the end of the war in Europe. It is also the story of thousands of men, most in their early twenties, many from the countries of the Commonwealth, on scores of squadrons, who sustained that offensive throughout the war - often at considerable cost in aircraft and crews.

Some aspects of the bomber offensive have aroused controversy, even hostility, but the facts are that from the fall of France in June 1940 until 1943 it was the only means Britain had of taking offensive action against the German homeland and its military capacity, and, ultimately it made a decisive contribution to winnimng the war.

During 1943 the United States 8th Air Force joined the offensive in growing numbers with daylight precision attacks. The scale and accuracy of Bomber Command's effort increased considerably helped by bigger bombs, new marking techniques, further radar navigational aids such as OBOE and H2S and a steady increase in the number of Lancasters. By April, 1944, when priority began to shift to preparation for "Overlord", Bomber Command could regularly despatch 700 or 800 heavy bombers in almost complete confidence that they would find and wreck their target areas. Individual Lancasters bombing at night using H2S were capable of greater accuracy than the USAAF B17s by day using formation precision bombing - there are examples of this in this book. But the Allied air offensive was facing immensely strengthened German air defences which were inflicting severe losses on the attacking bombers. Paradoxically it was the priority placed on air defence, which absorbed huge resources, that deprived the Luftwaffe of the offensive air power which would have played a crucial role in opposing the invasion of Normandy and the ground offensive on both the Western and Eastern fronts.

For the 8th Air Force the salvation was the advent of the long – range escort fighter, notably the P51 Mustang, which eventually achieved daylight air superiority over Western Europe. Bomber Command sought to contain its losses with technical developments such as "Window" and tactics, deceptive diversions and concentrations of overwhelming force against the principal targets.

That, then, was the situation which faced Arthur White and his colleagues when they joined 100 Squadron in the Autumn of 1944. The task must have seemed daunting - the tension clearly mounted as they ticked off each raid against the distant target of thirty required to complete an operational tour. But through turmoil and strain comes indomitable humour, the bonhomie, the precious personal memories of friends and family and the camaraderie which draws men together in combat. This crew was above all a team: highly trained, dedicated individuals expertly moulded and led by the "skipper" Dave Robb. Although survival in war owes much to chance, it was teamwork which increased the odds for this crew.

This book contains more than just an individual story. It is also a fascinating window on the Royal Air Force of the 1940s, the people and their lives, the jargon, the system which prepared and trained them for battle and the experiences which turned young men into veterans in a few short months. For those who were involved in Bomber Command it will, I am sure, bring back a flood of memories. For those who were not and for future historians it will be a valuable insight into a critical yet triumphant period in the history of the Royal Air Force.

John Herrington, C.B.
Air Vice Marshal R.A.F. (Retd.) 1991

Introduction

The idea for this story had been lurking at the back of my mind for a few months until, one day, I received a copy of a poem from Ian Reid, Secretary of the Waltham Association. It was to be another eighteen months or so before I managed to trace the writer, Mrs. Audrey Grealy, whose lines seemed to sum up my thoughts exactly – so much so, in fact, that I have headed the chapters which follow with verses from "Lancaster" although the sentiments expressed in the poem would equally apply to any other aircrew of Bomber Command. This is a point I wish to stress at the outset. Although this particular story is, primarily, about Lancaster crews the whole theme is about all the crews of Bomber Command.

"Lancaster", it seems, was published in the magazine, Lincolnshire Life, in September, 1982 at about the time that the Waltham Association held its first reunion. Waltham had been the home of 100 Squadron from 1942 to 1945 and Ian Reid, a young Post Office engineer, who had been fascinated by the tales of the local villagers about the war years, was determined to preserve the history and the legend of the unit by forming Waltham's own association. He was encouraged and supported in this by a group of former members of the Squadron and Station personnel who lived locally. Amongst these were Fred Bury, who worked in Intelligence, and two air gunners, John Prochera

1

and Jimmy Flynn. At the reunion of 1984 some thirty or forty ex Waltham "types" and their wives gathered to reminisce, shoot the odd line and sing the old songs and, at the Remembrance Service, to remember their old friends and colleagues on ops who had failed to make it.

And so, forty odd years on, one looks back at the war years and sees them in a new light. In view of the post war criticisms of the wartime bomber offensive it is useful to pause for a while to consider the achievements of Bomber Command and the context within which these achievements were made.

The role of Bomber Command and "Bomber" Harris's policy of area bombing has been the subject of heated controversy for the past forty five years and the debate will, no doubt, continue and intensify over the next few years as another "50th Anniversary" crops up.

Almost as soon as the war was over, that is, after the 1945 election, left wing politicians distanced themselves from Bomber Command. Harris himself was snubbed by being the only British Commander to be ignored in the Victory Honours List. Bomber crews were snubbed by the Government's refusal to award a Bomber Command Campaign Medal in recognition of their efforts and sacrifices. In fact, crews embarking on their tours of operations after "D" Day didn't even qualify for the Aircrew Europe Star but had to be content with the France and Germany Star which, as Harris is reported to have said, would be awarded to any clerk, butcher, baker and candle stick maker serving miles behind the fighting fronts.

Just what was it that brought this odium to Harris and Bomber Command? The short answer is that it was the moralising of left wing politicians, pacificists and so called intellectual arm chair historians. They were the people fortunate enough to fight World War 2 with the hindsight of ten, twenty or thirty years from the comfort of their 'Poly' or University common rooms and feed their views to "investigative journalists" of similar ilk who then swamped the media with their indignant outpourings. The facts of the matter are rather different. The only way to strike at Germany until "D" Day was by bombing German cities in order to destroy industrial potential and, hence, the war effort, and to demoralise the population. There was simply no other way. Even after "D" Day the strategic and tactical bombing offensive had to continue. As Field Marshall Montgomery said in a congratulatory message to Harris: "Your chaps made it easy for us."

By the early summer of 1940 Britain was standing alone to fight Hitler's Nazi Germany. Poland, Norway, Denmark, Holland and Belgium had been overrun by Hitler's Panzer divisions following the indiscriminate bombing of defenceless cities such as Warsaw and Rotterdam. France had surrendered yielding her Channel and Atlantic seaboards to the German conquerers. The British Expeditionary Force, consisting of some 300,000 men, had been miraculously evacuated from Dunkirk but its guns, tanks, transport – indeed all its equipment – had been left to rust on the Dunkirk beaches.

The Royal Navy was stretched to its limits attempting to protect the sea lanes of the world from the marauding "U" boats and "pocket battleships" of the German Navy. Simply to exist Britain had to import much of its food, all its oil, raw materials and war supplies from all over the world – particularly from America. It was the avowed aim of Hitler's "U" boat captains to blockade Britain and starve us into submission.

By June 1940 the only obstacle to Hitler's conquest of Britain was the Royal Air Force. "Operation Sealion," Hitler's code name for the invasion, required, first of all, the destruction of the R.A.F. which would be followed by the air and sea invasion of England. Less than thirty miles from Dover, all along the French Channel coast, thousands of German troops were gathered and ready to embark in boats and barges for the seaborne invasion. Just inland from these ports, in a huge semi circle reaching from Narvik in Norway, down the North Sea and the English Channel lay dozens of airfields which were the bases for Goering's Luftwaffe. On these airfields were based the fighters – Messerschmidt and Focke Wulf – which were intended to wipe out our Spitfires and Hurricanes; the Heinkels, Dorniers and Junkers which would bomb our bases to rubble and then mete out the same treatment to our ports and cities. And then there were the Stukas, the dive bombers, which, with the "U" boat packs, would smash our Home Fleet and then destroy its bases.

That was the scenario in the summer of 1940. London and Britain's major cities and ports were soon to burn; Coventry would be 'coventrated' whilst Goering whimsically flicked through his guide books to plan his terror, Baedaker' raids; 60,000 civilians were to die and many more thousands injured; children would be forced to leave their homes and their parents to seek safety in less industrialised areas and one million homes would be destroyed or damaged.

In those days one hoped that America would join us in the struggle but we couldn't rely on that because of the strong isolationist feeling in the States at that time. Russia was still Germany's ally and was to remain so for another year. Mussolini, in his grandiose phrase, "The Pact of Steel," allied Italy with Germany to get what pickings he could in North Africa. This left Britain with another front to defend in order to safeguard the Suez Canal and, hence, our communications with India, Australia and New Zealand.

There remained ourselves, our cousins from the Commonwealth and the free forces who had managed to escape from Hitler's Europe but the only way to strike at, what was now called "Fortress Europe", was from the air. Hence, a long term strategy had been evolved whereby Germany would be reduced by a long war of attrition – a war fought in the air. Before that could happen, however, new four engined bombers, the Stirling, Halifax and Lancaster were to come off the drawing

4

boards and, eventually, augment and, later, replace the Whitleys, Hampdens and Wellingtons. New navigational aids such as "Gee", "H2S" and "Oboe" which were to concentrate hundreds or, even, a thousand bombers over German cities had to be invented and produced in their thousands. New bomb sights were developed to aim the new bombs such as the 4000lb. "cookie", the 12000lb. Tallboy the 22000lb. "Grand Slam" not to mention the vicious little incendiaries which were to rain over Germany in their tens or hundreds of thousands.

All that, however, was to lie in the future. In that summer of 1940 the people of Britain braced themselves for the Nazi onslaught. They already knew what to expect because Hitler had made no secret of the new rules of war – "Total War" – the "Blitzkrieg." Newsreels had already shown us the effects of bombing on undefended cities such as Warsaw and Rotterdam. In fact, Germany had practised it all before by the bombing of Guernica in the Spanish Civil War. The newsreels had also shown the plight of thousands of refugees fleeing the towns, villages and cities before the advancing Panzers and being gunned down by the Messerschmidts and Focke Wulfs of the Luftwaffe.

The glorious "Few" of Fighter Command spared us that. Day after day through August and September, 1940, these men in their Spitfires and Hurricanes battled against hundreds and hundreds of German bombers intent on destroying, first, their bases and then London and the Channel ports. Escorted by hundreds of fighters they came in wave after wave, day after day, week after week taking tremendous toll. But the toll on the would be invaders was far greater. With Fighter Command reduced to its last reserves by the 15th September the Luftwaffe was defeated and demoralised. Battle of Britain Day remains to remind us of our debt to the "Few" who, through their sheer dedication and valour, saved us from invasion.

Whilst Fighter Command was fighting the Lufwaffe in the air Whitleys, Hampdens and Wellingtons of Bomber Command were pounding the invasion ports. Their targets were the massing German troops, armour, invasion barges, supplies and the communications systems of Northern France. By October the combined operations of Fighter and Bomber Commands had been so effective that "Operation Sealion", Hitler's code name for the invasion had been called off. We now had that vital breathing space in which Bomber Command could re-equip so that by May, 1942, Air Chief Marshall Sir Arthur Harris could launch his first 1,000 bomber raid on Cologne.

This story is not about such famous airmen as the Dambusters of 617 Squadron who were in a class of their own. Nor is it intended to repeat the ideas and excellently researched subject matter of Len Deighton's "Bomber". It is the story of all the anonymous crews of Bomber Command told through the experiences of an ordinary Lancaster crew and some of their pals in other crews who managed to complete a tour of thirty operations when the initial odds against doing this were in the order of six or seven to one against although, as crews gained experience, the odds did shorten to two to one! It was the anonymous crews of Bomber Command who dropped a million tons of bombs on Germany; it was they who made such newspaper headlines as '1000 Bombers Blast Ruhr' or, tucked away in the inside pages, '25 of our aircraft failed to return' or it might have been 10 or, in the case of Nurenburg, 94. In every one of those aircraft there were seven young men. The balance sheet of their efforts shows, on the credit side:

1 million tons of bombs dropped on Germany.
50,000 mines laid in German harbours and shipping lanes.
60% of German cities devastated.
Further bombing of Britain prevented by forcing Germany to build fighters for its own defence.
Destruction of hundreds of German "U" boats either in harbour, under construction or in component form at inland factories.

Chaotic dislocation of the Continental transport system.
The provision of invaluable support to all the allied armies
   advancing into Germany after "D" Day.

Particularly important, although not generally recognised, was
the invaluable help given to Russia by the diversion of German
war production from the Russian front to the defence of the
Fatherland. Tens of thousand of anti tank guns destined for use
against Russia were diverted to German cities where they put
up the deadly box barrages of flak to destroy our attacking
bomber forces. Right from Germany's invasion of Russia in
1941 Stalin had badgered Churchill and Roosevelt for a second
front. It was Bomber Command that supplied that second front
and it was Albert Speer, the German Minister of Production,
who made that assertion.

But the last, although not the least, entry on this side of the
balance sheet was the intangible effect on the morale of the
British people. After the blitzes of 1940 and 1941 British men,
women and children could listen to the laboured drone of
hundreds of "ours" climbing on course with their deadly loads
for delivery to Hitler's Germany. Many of these men, women
and children, living near a bomber airfield, would count the
'planes taking off – and count them again on their return. Next
morning they would learn, with grim satisfaction, from radio
or newspaper, the details of last night's raid:

"It was Essen last night – nineteen missing."

Many an airman could tell the story of the old lady or the old
chap in the pub:

"Here you are lad, have this one on me and, the next time you
go, drop one for me as well.!"

On the debit side of the balance sheet was the loss of over
50,000 aircrew. Thousands more were wounded by flak, cannon
or machine gun fire. Many, now members of the illustrious
"Guinea Pig Club", saw with horror their charred hands and

7

arms, burnt to the bone by fire in the aircraft thousands of feet above the earth. Many more were disfigured by facial burns and all of them owe their lives and their very reason to the wonderful work of Sir Archibald McKindoe and his team of plastic surgeons. There were two other "clubs" which many aircrew were qualified to join – the Caterpillar Club and the Goldfish Club. Shot up over Fortress Europe a skillful skipper might just manage to give his crew and himself the opportunity to bail out. If you ever see an elderly chap wearing a little gold caterpillar on his tie or lapel you are looking at someone who did just that. Similarly, a skipper might just have managed to "ditch" his stricken bomber in the sea. By going through the disciplined drill of "ditching" the crew might just manage to climb into the dinghy before the aircraft sank. Such airmen, rescued after probably several days in the North Sea or English Channel, may be recognised by the insignia of a little gold fish. They are members of the Goldfish Club.

Who were these young men? Audrey Grealy in "Lancaster" gives part of the answer:

"Lads who were bank clerks and milkmen and teachers, carpenters, lawyers and grocers and peers."They were the lads you went to school with; served your apprenticeship with; had your first fag or pint with; they were the crews of "Main Force". There were over 100,000 of them. They came from Britain, Canada, Australia, New Zealand, South Africa, Rhodesia. They came from Poland, Holland, France, Norway – indeed any country that valued freedom – to make up the crews of Bomber Command. When peace finally came in May, 1945, only half of them were left.

They did not regard themselves as heroes, although their deeds were heroic, but they were proud of the brevets they wore. Each crew was the best in the Flight; their Flight was the best on the Squadron; their squadron was the best in the group and their group the best in Bomber Command. They were young; they were carefree; they lived for the day. Within a crew their comradeship was unique. They trusted each other implicitly. They lived together, ate together, drank together, flew together and, all too often, they died together. Just a bunch of lads trying to get through a tour. I suppose you could call them the "Bread and Butter Bomber Boys."

Chapter One:

Memories

Where are the bombers, the Lancs on the runway,
Black faced and roaring, snub nosed and dour;
Full up with aircrew and window and ammo
And dirty great cookies to drop on the Ruhr?

Chance, fate, coincidence, call it what you may, plays a strange part in life. After World War 2 50,000 surviving aircrew returned to R.A.F. stores and handed in their kit for ever. Life was no longer ordered for them by reveille, roll calls, parades and going into action. For the former aircrew there were, no longer, the calls to briefing and the tension of preparing for ops. No longer was there that strange ambivalence of emotions – one half hoping that the op would take place leaving one less to do, whilst the other half hoped for a 'stand down' so that there could be a night out on the town.

After six years of war they were starting a new life in 'Civvie Street' in the brave new world they had done so much to win. Pilots, navigators, bomb aimers, flight engineers, wireless operators and air gunners would return to their peace time jobs of bank clerks, teachers, carpenters, clerks, engineers, firemen, policemen or any one of a thousand occupations far removed from the excitement, glamour and horror of Bomber Command. Some would resume their pre-war studies, apprenticeships or training interrupted by the war whilst a few more would continue their flying careers either in the R.A.F. itself or in civil aviation.

For most of them there had been no period of adolescence – that time in life when one serves his apprenticeship and makes his mistakes without too many repercussions and, in short, learns to grow up. Almost overnight, it seemed, boys turned into men. There were few opportunities in the post war world for pilots; fewer still for navigators and wireless operators and literally none for air bombers and air gunners. The cohesion of the crew and comradeship of the squadron were dispersed and gone for ever. Young lads were now men with jobs, wives and families to worry about. They had returned to a Britain beleagured by austerity instead of air raids; they had returned to a Britain impoverished by war – to a Britain of rations and shortages but to a Britain that was still the best because they had helped to prove it.

They had to learn to adjust to the new life in Civvie Street and, for many, this was not easy. Some managed to pick up the threads of their old, pre war job but many others found that aircrew categories and a tour of ops were no qualifications for the jobs on offer in post war Britain and so they had to start again – at the bottom. And so, for thirty or forty years, they made their separate ways in life. They embarked on new careers, gained promotion, some emigrated, some switched careers, some fell by the wayside and some of them died. Slowly, memories of the war years faded. Momentarily they were awakened by a chance meeting with an old 'oppo' or, maybe, a war film. Perhaps it was a new book, a letter in a newspaper, Remembrance Day or Battle of Britain Sunday. A few, of course. were fortunate enough to keep the old memories alive by regular, organised reunions.

For most, however, there comes a time in life when there is actually time for nostalgia. Perhaps it comes at the end of working life when the kids have grown up, the mortgage paid off, retirement looming ahead and there is time to think about the old days. This mental search could be sparked off by any one of a thousand things – for me it was sparked off by a Lancaster.

On a sunny, Saturday afternoon in August, 1980, there was to be a gala in the local park in Dewsbury. The highlight of the afternoon was to be a fly past by the Battle of Britain Memorial Flight during which the last, airworthy, surviving Lancaster, "City of Lincoln", would make a bombing run over the park followed by a similar appearance by a Victor "V" bomber. Sitting in the garden, just two or three hundred yards from the park, Paddy and I chatted with Margaret and Ken Booth, two neighbours from across the road. Over the tannoy from the nearby park could be heard the commentary of the afternoon's events. Sipping a cold beer during a lull in the commentary Ken suddenly remarked:

"I think I can hear them."

The four of us turned to search the sky to the east and then, far away in the distance, came the first, faint sound of aero engines. This was not the whistling whine of jets but the deep throated growl of Merlins. It was the sound we had lived with in the 'forties' – it had been a part of life that could never be forgotten. Now, almost forty years later, we heard it again. Slowly, at first, three 'planes came into view – like three tiny models in the distance. Then, almost too quickly, it seemed, before we had time to savour the sight, that gracious, old lady Lancaster appeared more rapidly escorted by a Hurricane and a Spitfire. About half a mile away the escort peeled off and "City of Lincoln" advanced alone, proudly, confidently and majestically at about 800 ft.

The sound increased rapidly reaching a crescendo as she passed over the house at 200 knots. The spectators' heads turned 180 degrees as she banked behind the church displaying her profile like a coquettish young maiden. Momentarily she

13

"City of Lincoln" Over Dewsbury.

disappeared behind the trees as she went to display her charms to the eager observers in the park. The Merlins' roar subsided in the distance but then she returned again and now she was the deadly war Lancaster sweeping around the park prior to lining up for her bombing run. The sound became a roar that rattled windows and tiles as she raced in from the north with bomb doors open like the jaws of death. Today, the bomb bay was empty – forty years ago it would have housed seven tons of cookies, incendiaries or high explosives. Once again she headed south to complete her mission and then, bomb doors closed, she banked and turned again for a proud, final pass whilst the Spitfire and Hurricane took up station to escort the old girl home. As she passed overhead one could sense the pride and see the beauty of the finest bomber ever built. Quickly, now, she disappeared into the East and the sound of the Merlins faded but even as she vanished from sight the sound still lingered on. The watchers were left, at last, remembering. To her friends she was beautiful, graceful, docile, loving and loyal; to her enemies she was deadly, ruthless, vengeful and implacable.

For a few moments there was a strange silence just time to flash back in time to those days when, to actually fly in a Lanc was almost routine. There was just time to wonder, to ponder, to muse and to remember when the silence was suddenly shattered by a roar and a crack of sound more fearful than an overhead thunderclap. The shadow of an enormous moth flashed overhead as a Victor "V" bomber made its pass over the park to conclude the afternoon's programme and disappeared in an instant.

So there it was – two vastly different bombers from two vastly different eras; one from the old generation and one from the new. Yet it was the "old girl" that brought tears to the eyes of men and women alike. Those who had lived through the war years would remember the sight and the sound of hundreds of them and their memories were passed on to their children building up the legend. A lady in her early sixties summed it all up at a recent squadron reunion when "City of Lincoln" made a brief appearance:

"Yes," she said, "I shall always remember that sound." The Lancaster's engineer replied:

"I agree. The Lanc has that special sound – all the others make a noise!"

That evening I started to think back. On a wall in my study hangs a photograph of seven, smiling young men standing in front of Lancaster "M2" in which they had just completed the last operation of their tour. Standing on the back row is Flying Officer Elmer Mosure, R.C.A.F., or "Mo", the bomb aimer. Mo was a typical, tough, six foot Canadian from the Pacific Coast and, at the age of thirty five, was the the "Daddy" of the crew. Next to him stands Squadron Leader David Robb, or "Robbie", the skipper who was twenty six and hailed from Winnipeg. Robbie wore the red and white ribbon of the Air Force Cross and, within minutes of the photograph being taken, both he and Mo were to learn that they had been awarded the Distinguished Flying Cross. Next to Robbie is myself, the navigator of the crew. Prior to enlisting in the R.A.F. I had worked in the family business of wool merchants in Bradford. At the end of the row stands Flight Sergeant Arthur Gamble our flight engineer who came from Pudsey. To avoid confusion between the two Arthurs Robbie and Mo had christened the flight engineer "Poker" and "Poker" he remained. In typical North American fashion the two Arthurs were abbreviated to "Art".

Squatting at the front of the photograph are the three other members of the crew. On the left is a lithe, nineteen year old from Innisfail, Alberta, Pilot Officer Bob Gibson, or "Gibby",the rear gunner. In the centre is Flight Sergeant Ronnie Brown, aged twenty, the wireless operator from Chester le Street, Co. Durham. The group is completed by another young Canadian, Pilot

Officer Monty Kerr, also nineteen from Ottawa. Monty is the mid upper gunner.

Two other bits of memorabilia could be seen in the study. There was a painting of a Lancaster taking off at dusk entitled "Night Raid For Jug and Bottle and Crew." We had liked to think that "J Jig", christened "Jug and Bottle", was our very own Lanc in those days having flown, perhaps, half of our tour in her. The painting was a Christmas present from my daughter, Jane. The other piece of memorabilia was an Airfix model of Lancaster "A Able" or "Able Mabel" as her skipper had christened her. By a strange coincidence we had flown in "Able Mabel" and she was one of the few Lancasters to 'get a century' – actually completeing 132 operations. "Able Mabel" was Flight Lieutenant Jack Playford's 'plane for his tour and his crew literally nurtured it. Woe betide any crew that took liberties with their 'kite'.

Further rummaging around produced my innoculation record, log book, and Air Ministry text on Air Navigation – the navigator's Bible in those days – a few old snapshots and some formal group photographs. There were groups from training days at Stratford on Avon, East London and Queenstown in South Africa and a few old, indistinct snaps of some of the crew with a couple of W.A.A.F. friends on the squadron. There was the last Station Bulletin from R.A.F. Grimsby with "Groupie's" exhortation: "Good luck! Good bombing! and No early returns!"

And that was all there was to show for five years of life in the Royal Air Force – the training, the travel, the waiting and the Squadron. How did it all begin?

17

Chapter Two

Putting the Jigsaw Together

Where are the pilots, the navs and airgunners,
Wops and bomb aimers and flight engineers;
Lads who were bank clerks and milkmen and
    teachers,
Carpenters, lawyers and grocers and peers?

It was to be another two years before fate decided to fill in another piece of the jigsaw. Pat Howard, one of my teaching colleagues and her husband, Pete, moved to Waltham, near Grimsby. Pete, knowing of my wartime association with Waltham, sent me a copy of the "Grimsby Evening Telegraph" which carried an article describing the first reunion of the Waltham Association. Membership of this association was open to all who had served on the station during World War 2 and included station personnel and members of 142 and 100 Squadrons.

The association had been set up by John Prochera and Jimmy Flynn, who had served on 100 Squadron, and Ian Reid, a young Post Office engineer. Following my application for membership I learned for the first time of the Aircrew Association which was soon to open a branch in Bradford. I later resumed my membership of the Royal Air Forces Asociation and, through "Intercom" and "Airmail", the publications of the A.C.A. and

R.A.F.A., memories of the war years started to trickle back. The breakthrough came in May, 1984, when my wife, Paddy, and I spent a weekend at the Crown Hotel in Framlingham, Suffolk. The choice of Framlingham itself for the weekend was entirely fortuitous – our sole reason for the choice was that Suffolk was a county we had never previously visited.

Over coffee, one evening, we chatted with a couple of our age, Mr. & Mrs. Maurice Baker. As is usual in such conversations we asked about each others home towns and, in Maurice's case, we found they lived near Newport, Monmouth. When I remarked that I once had a very good friend, Goff Attewell, who came from Magor, near Newport, Maurice exclaimed that he lived in the same town as Goff and taught Goff's children at school. Amazed and delighted at this news I gave him my address and 'phone number which he promised to pass on to Goff in a few day's time. It was forty years since I had last seen Goff and I could hardly wait to meet up with him again. In the event it was to be another five months before we actually met again.

In September, Paddy and I went to the reunion at Waltham which was held in the Crest Hotel. It was a strange feeling, walking towards the lounge, wondering who we would meet up with after all those years. Young, uniformed aircrew in their late teens and early twenties would now be greying, balding, elderly chaps in blazers, tweed jackets or lounge suits. How would we recognise each other? Slowly, entering in ones and twos, the lounge began to fill. A tall white haired, distinguished looking gentleman called out:

"Are there any navigators here? Anyone remember George Pirie?" I walked up to him and introduced myself. Squadron Leader George Pirie, D.F.C., had been the Station Navigation Officer at Waltham in my time and it was he who had taken a particular interest in training his navigators in the use of H2S – of which, more later.

We shook hands: "Art White," I said, "Dave Robb's crew."

"Robbie!" he exclaimed, "How's the boozy old devil going on?"Robbie, George and other section leaders had been great pals in the Waltham days and there was many a tale of drinking competitions in the Mess. Little wonder that when we eventually got a 'plane we felt we could call our own it was named 'Jug and Bottle' although, in actual fact, it was named after the out-sales department of a Doncaster pub. Three "Bills" joined us – Hartnett, Hancock and Evans. We had all been on the squadron together in '44 and, as we chatted together, memories came trickling back.

In another corner of the lounge, sitting round a table covered with pint glasses, was a group of five or six. It was Ian Smith with most of his crew! How remarkable it was that, after all these years they should be able to get together again! Standing at the bar, drinking a blackcurrant and lemonade, was another tall, silver haired figure who seemed vaguely familiar. Someone introduced us – he was Stamper Metcalfe, bomb aimer in Flight Sergeant Henry Brown's crew. They had usually flown Lancaster "H How" and Stamper had spent many hours painting the name "Hellzapoppin" on its nose. As we shall see later we flew our fourth operation in Hellzapoppin with disastrous consequences for the 'plane. When Stamper realised who I was he grabbed my arm and announced to all and sundry:"Hey! This is one of the rotten buggers who wrote off our kite!"

Around 7.30 we assembled for the dinner party where we met and chatted with other ex aircrew and ground staff – fitters, cooks, WAAF transport drivers and many others. After dinner we watched a video, 'Night Bombers', which is the only colour version of a full Lancaster operation. Such a reunion wouldn't be complete without a sing song round the piano and so, once again, we bawled out the old squadron songs with as much gusto as we had done forty years earlier.

On the Sunday morning we drove a couple of miles to the village hall at Holton le Clay which lies just across the road from the end of the old runway. The villagers greeted us like old friends and, after coffee and biscuits, we made our way back to the main Grimsby – Louth road to a small clearing which lies between the road and a row of trees which bounded the runway. Here, in a little green oasis, is a simple granite memorial stone dedicated to those who lost their lives serving with 100 Squadron. The stone carries the skull and crossbones of the Squadron Crest and, below, the Squadron motto from its Singapore days: "Sarang Tebuan Jangan Dijolok" which means "Do not stir up the hornets' nest". The memorial was erected by the Royal Observer Corps, 'Bravo 3 Post'. Following a moving memorial service and the laying of wreaths, which ended the reunion, we made our farewells and began to disperse with reminders and exhortations to meet again next year. Altogether it was a moving occasion and the nostalgia deepened as Paddy and I drove down to the old airfield.

Little remained – the control tower which we had 'shot up' with Verey pistols as we left Waltham for Elsham Wolds in April, 1945, stood looking neglected and forlorn. Forty years ago it was manned by flying control officers and WAAFS who had directed a couple of dozen Lancasters from dispersal to runway to take off. Hours later, on their return, skippers would call up "Shopboy" and we would hear their welcoming voices giving directions and permision to land. Where once there had been a little township of Nissen huts which had been home to hundreds of airmen and airwomen there remained one rusty Nissen. Where once there had been Flight offices, section offices, administration buildings, the ops room, crew room, parachute section, officers, sergeants and airmen's messes there remained two or three wooden frame huts. There they stood – windowless with an odd door hanging on by an odd hinge – with dried leaves and dust idly swirling around in the light afternoon breeze. It was impossible to identify them. "Is that the old ablutions block?" "What happened to our Nissen?"

We walked across a patch of lank grass to a wide, tarmacced stretch – the old main runway. Weeds grew through the cracked surface giving an overall picture of neglect and decay. After a final look round, with a strange feeling of sadness and loss, we drove back to the memorial which was at the far end of the short runway. Forty years ago there had been a little shack where one could buy a mug of tea, a snack and a newspaper. There was still the line of trees bordering the edge of the runway which often left some of their twigs from the upper branches in the undercarriage of a Lanc which had been a bit late in clearing them with its full bomb load.

That, more or less, was the end of the weekend. I returned home with a squadron tie, car sticker, plans of the airfield and a copy of "Lancaster." On arrival at home I found an event had occurred which went some way to completing the jigsaw. My daughter informed me that Goff had 'phoned. Maurice Baker had carried my 'phone number around for almost three months

Goff

and forgotten about it. However, late in August, he had met Goff and gave it to him as he was about to go on holiday. That night I 'phoned Goff and we had a long chat about the old days."Incidentally Art," he said, "there was a call out for you in 'Airmail.' " He read out the message from Dave Robb in Canada who was visiting England and hoped to look up the three English members of his crew: Art (Poker) Gamble, the flight engineer, Ronnie Brown, wireless operator and myself, the navigator. Unfortunately, by this time, Robbie had been and gone but, nevertheless, I now had an address to write to and within a couple of weeks I had a reply giving me news of the Canadian branch of the crew – Gibby and Monty, the gunners and Mo, our bomb aimer.

My next task was to find Poker and Ronnie. I wrote to a number of newspapers both locally and in the North East and within three days I had a telephone call. It was from Poker who was living a bare twenty miles away, near Doncaster, and he had seen my letter in the 'Yorkshire Post.' Two other callers told me that they knew him and mentioned his place of work. A few days later I had a number of calls from the Durham area from friends of Ronnie. Sadly, they reported that Ronnie had died, after a long illness,in 1976. The wonderful thing was that, without exception, they spoke highly of him, of his loyalty and friendship. There could be no higher tribute to Ronnie than the fact, that after more than eight years, he was so clearly remembered and missed by his friends. Amongst the last of the calls was one from one of Ronnie's cousins who was calling on behalf of her mother, Ronnie's aunt, now a lady getting on in years. 'Auntie', it seems, had been a second mother to Ronnie and she told me that he spent most of his wartime leaves with her. From her I learned that Ron had a son, Jim, who, at that time, was the Squadron Engineering Officer of the Red Arrows. News of my search reached Jim and I had a very moving letter from him with a copy of Ron's log book.

Meanwhile, I was reunited with Goff at Usk, Gwent, in October, 1984. We had a memorable weekend with him and his wife, Rosemary, when we chatted on into the small hours about our times together training in South Africa and our Air Force and post war careers. We planned to meet again at Christmas but this, sadly, was not to be. Goff died suddenly of a heart attack in early December. We had been close friends for over a year and, even with a gap of forty years, he died a good friend. But for him this story could never have been written. Of all the men I have ever met Goff was the epitome of a good sport, a good friend and an English gentleman.

Following close upon this sad news was the event which was to reunite me with both Robbie and the Squadron. This was the occasion on the 14th December, 1984, when the Squadron was to be presented with its new Standard. Through announcements in 'Intercom', 'Airmail' and the Waltham Association ex members of the Squadron were invited to the ceremony. Poker and I drove down to R.A.F. Wyton where the squadron was now flying Canberras after the post war years on Lincolns and, later, the Victor "V" bombers. We booked into an hotel at St. Ives and the first person we met was "Ziggy" Zaggerman, the bombing leader in our time, now turned 70 with a heart by-pass but as lively as the last time we had seen him forty years ago. *Ziggy* and I had done an op together to the oil refinery at Bottrop when we made up a crew for the Squadron Commander. With him was George Pirie, my old 'Nav boss', and a dozen or so others including Bill Hartnett and Bill Hancock who were navigators on the Squadron when I was there.

A liaison officer had been appointed to take us to Wyton and to brief us on the format of the ceremony including when and when not to wear medals. We then made our way to the airfield where we were directed to a hangar in which the ceremony was to take place. The hangar, which had been newly painted for the occasion, seemed enormous. In one corner stood a Canberra whilst, at the other side was a First World War Avro. In the centre was a dais, the saluting base, and, at the front of the hangar, were five or six rows of chairs for the guests.

The Squadron marched on to parade to "Eagle Squadron" played by the band of the Royal Air Force College, Cranwell, under the direction of Flight Lieutenant D. Wood. This was followed by the marching on of the Old Standard to "Point of War." The Presenting Officer, Marshall of the Royal Air Force Sir Michael Beetham, GCB,CBE, DFC,AFC,FRAeS, arrived at the saluting base to be greeted by a General Salute after which he inspected the parade. Then, to the strains of 'Auld Lang Syne', there were two or three nostalgic minutes as the Old Standard was marched out of sight when quite a few of us found our eyes watering!

Following the uncasing of the New Standard was the blessing by the Venerable G.R. Renowden after which Sir Michael received the New Standard from the Station Commander, Group Captain N.B. Baldwin, R.A.F. Sir Michael then formally presented the New Standard and addressed the Squadron and the guests.

In his address Sir Michael recalled the Squadron's history and the battle honours depicted on the Standard. It was remarkable that, among the guests, there was someone associated with each of the battle honours. One grand old gentleman had flown Fe 2Bs and Handley Page 0-400s in 1917 when 100 Squadron became the first designated night bomber squadron; two fitters were associated with the Squadron's Vildebeests in Malaya when the Squadron was virtually annihilated by the Japanese at Singapore in 1942 and, of course, there was a sprinkling of Lancaster crews from the Waltham days.

Following Sir Michael's address the New Standard was marched on to the Parade to the 'National Anthem' and then trooped in front of the Squadron. Embroidered in gold, on each side of the Squadron crest with its blue background, were the

The New Standard. Photo: 100 Squadron

Squadron's battle honours:Ypres 1917; Somme 1918; Independent Force and Germany 1918; Malaya 1941 – 1942; Fortress Europe 1943 – 1944; Ruhr 1943 – 1945; Berlin 1943 – 1945; Normandy 1944.Then, after the General Salute, the Squadron marched off to the march we were all familiar with, "The Royal Air Force March Past."

Wonderful as the ceremony was, it was surpassed by the welcome, hospitality and courtesy of the Squdron Commander, Wing Commander M.J. Purdie and his Canberra crews. It wasn't until the ceremony was over that Poker and I first saw Robbie. He had been sitting on the front row with the 'top brass' and had already been at Wyton for two days. But he was the same old Robbie – a little older of course, plumper and balder but with the same drive, verve and capacity for beer that he had in the old days. We crept up behind him and tapped his shoulder."Art! Poker! Gee you guys haven't changed a bit! Well, I guess Art's lost some of his hair but who am I to talk? Wasn't that show just great? C'mon I want you to meet ......"He dragged us off to the Champagne reception where he introduced us to the Squadron C.O. who, in turn, introduced us to Sir Michael and then things really started to happen.

First we walked over to inspect the New Standard which seemed to give us a sense of belonging as we had been closely involved in two of the Honours – "Battle of the Ruhr" and "Fortress Europe" when we took part in the follow up to Normandy supporting the allied armies advancing into Germany. We were joined by Ziggy and George Pirie and then we were literally beseiged by 1984 Canberra crews. They really wanted to know what it was all about in World War 2. What was the flak really like? How did we cope with enemy fighters? What sort of things went wrong and what did we do about them and how did we feel about it all?

The rest of the weekend can be imagined! We met a lot of old 'oppos' (wartime colleagues), drank a lot of beer and heard and

27

The Duisburg Ops Board. Photo: I.W.M.

shot a lot of lines! One highlight of the day was a replica of the Squadron 'Ops Board' for the 14th October, 1944. This showed the battle order for the day when we made two attacks on Duisburg within twenty four hours. The Deputy Director of the Imperial War Museum photographed a group of us who had taken part in the raids standing by the ops board pointing to our entries.

In the evening we all attended a party in the Officers Mess where the whole process continued. In a corner of the mess during a session with Robbie and the Wing Commander the 100 Squadron Association was conceived and, a year later, it was born. The Squadron did us oldies proud making us feel forty years younger and a foot taller. The evening came to a close with half a dozen of us getting around the piano and singing the Squadron song – 1944 style! The fact that Ziggy and Robbie, two of the characters in the song, were actually there particularly tickled the young crews and their wives and girl friends.

Robbie spent three days with us in Dewsbury before flying back home to Canada and, during that time, he, Poker and I reminisced and talked about the old days and the other members of the crew and a few more pieces of the jigsaw slipped into place. In May, 1985, Monty came over as the Ottawa representative of those who took part in the "Manna" operations which had been our last trip. Monty and Gibby, who came over for the 1985 Waltham reunion, filled in one or two more pieces and also gave me snippets of news about Mo. It seems that Mo, unfortunately, was almost a recluse back at his home in Sooke, B.C. and had put the war years firmly behind him. Mo's war had been one of revenge – revenge for a brother killed in France the shock of which killed his father a few days later. Mo felt that he had to do what he did and, with the end of the war, that was that.

In 1987 I heard that Georgie, Robbie's wife, was terminally ill from cancer and Robbie, quite naturally, was distraught. I

29

First Reunion of 100 Sqdn. Association. Photo: 100 Squadron.

had never met Georgie although we had corresponded on the odd occasion and chatted on the 'phone. For some strange reason I felt that I ought to pay a visit and in April I flew out to Toronto. I spent a couple of days there and visited Georgie in hospital. Robbie and I had a few beers together in the evenings and, again, we chatted about the old days. Gibby came over from Ottawa and drove me back to his home where I met up with Monty again. He and Monty showed me the sights and threw a party where I met a few more oppos from the Squadron days and, from them, gleaned a few more snippets which help to fill in the gaps.

After two days in Ottawa I flew out to Victoria with the principal aim of seeing Mo. He and I had worked closely together in the crew and, crusty though he might turn out to be, I felt I had to see him for myself. I was met at Victoria airport by Ron "Doc" Watson, another former Canadian colleague on the Squadron, and his wife, Rosemary. Their hospitality and, indeed, that of all the Canadians I met, was out of this world but that is another story. It was Doc who drove me out to see Mo. We followed the coast until we reached the little township of Sooke and then turned off to the right along a maple tree lined road. A couple of hundred yards or so along the road stood Mo's house so we pulled into the driveway, got out of the car and knocked on the door.

There was no answer and no sign of Mo although we could hear a dog barking in the distance so we took a turn around the garden which was really an acre of grass, half a dozen maple trees, two large and one smaller outbuildings. We tried the largest first and were greeted by a large, fussy, welcoming dog of, predominantly, Dalmation ancestry and named, aptly enough, "Domino."

"Anyone here?" called out Doc.

"Yeah – who's that?" came a slow, deep drawl.

We walked into, what transpired to be, Mo's workshop. Take away the battered baseball cap and the grimy overalls and there was the same Mo I had last seen forty two years ago wearing the uniform of Flying Officer Mosure D.F.C., R.C.A.F. – except that he was now seventy eight years old. True, he had a slight stoop and the short, bristly hair was now a steely grey but they were the same clear, blue eyes set in the same leathery, tanned face. He stared at us for a moment and recognised Doc from a previous meeting. Looking again at me he paused for another few moments and then:

"Is that you Art? How in hell did you get here? Did you fly out here? I haven't been in one of them goddam things since I left the squadron! The hell with them all!"

Embracing him and then holding him at arm's length I replied:"Well, you old devil, I've written and written to you but never a word in reply so I thought I'd come out to see what you're up to!"

"Oh Gee Art," he answered, "I never write letters. I've got that godammed arthritis in my fingers. Anyway, Art, you don't have to go worrying about me. I'm O.K. here and there's plenty to keep me busy."

For the next hour he showed us around his workshop which housed the most comprehensive set of tools and machinery imaginable including lathes, drills and welding equipment with which he seemed to spend most of his time making and repairing things for himself and his neighbours. Outside, in another outhouse, stood a tractor as clean and shiny as a show room car.

"Why do you need a tractor Mo?" I asked. He looked at me as though I was bit thick.

"Why do I need a tractor? Come along here." He led us down the field and pointed to an enormous root ball of a maple tree.

"How in hell did that get there?" he asked. "The tractor!" He then took us to his boundary hedge and pointed to his neighbour's garden. A few yards away was a swimming pool with a landscaped banking which provided shelter from the prevailing wind.

32

"How in hell did all that dirt get up there? he asked again. "The tractor!"

A further tour of his property revealed a Ford truck which he had completely rebuilt and reconditioned. Bought for a few dollars as scrap it was now worth several thousand dollars although he had no intention of selling it even though he had another truck for his everyday needs.

He then took us into his house – a warm, spacious and comfortable bungalow where, over coffee and biscuits, he described how he had built and fitted it out himself in his spare time. He also described how he had built himself a cabin cruiser and how he had acquired and reconditioned a Packard engine to power it. In the two or three hours we spent with him he would say very little about the squadron days except to raise hell with me for, allegedly, instructing Robbie to take the 'plane in too low on our food dropping trip to Rotterdam."You know, Art," he said, "that aiming point came up pretty godamm fast at 500 feet!" When I tried to get more details of some of our ops he simply remarked that if I had seen half the things that he had seen it would have scared the shit out of me. For the rest of the time he and Doc had a complicated discussion comparing the Lanc with the American Flying Fortress – the B.17 – and the respective merits, or otherwise, of the American Norden bomb sight and our own Mark 14.

Just before we left he called me over to the fireplace and picked up a photograph."Have you any grandchildren Art?" I replied that I had two granddaughters. He showed me the photograph: "Yeah, but you sure as hell aint got what I've got. That's my great grandson!"Doc took our photographs after which we embraced and left. Mo, as mentioned, will never write letters but I call him now and again if the 'phone bill hasn't been too heavy.

And so, with some parts of the jigsaw still missing, the picture may never be really complete. Perhaps, as I continue writing, a few more pieces will fall into place. We shall see.

Chapter Three

EARLY DAYS

Geordies and Cocknies and Wiltshire Moonrakers,
Little dark men from the valleys of Wales,
Manxmen, Devonians, Midlanders, Scouses,
Jocks from the Highlands and Tykes from the Dales.

Before the outbreak of war Britain already had conscription from the age of eighteen and as the war progressed it was extended up the age range to the early forties. Of the three services the R.A.F. was probably the the most attractive to young lads. It was the youngest service and, by its very nature, did not have the 'footslogging' connotation of the Army. The majority of R.A.F. personnel performed a wide range of skilled jobs from engineering, electrical, radio and a score of allied trades, to operational control and intelligence work. Their main purpose was to keep the aircraft flying and it has been said that for every man in the air ten were needed on the ground. The uniform was regarded by many as the most attractive of the services and, very early on, members of the R.A.F. were dubbed 'Brylcreem Boys.' However, it is a fact that the R.A.F. attracted more than its fair share of skilled men and women and could afford to be more selective in its intake. The only category of servicemen who could not be conscripted was aircrew. All aircrew – pilots, navigators, bomb aimers,air gunners, wireless operators and flight engineers were volunteers. Men who had exemption from military service, such as farmers, for example, could only join the forces as aircrew. Goff was just one of thousands of those in 'reserved occupations' who found that to be the only way of 'doing their bit'.

What was it that compelled tens of thousands of lads in their late 'teens to volunteer for aircrew? Strange though it may seem to us in the 1990s the average person in the '30s very rarely even saw an aeroplane! Of course, we saw them regularly on films at the cinema; in the '20s and '30s pioneers such as Charles Lindburgh, Amy Johnson, Mollison, Campbell and Black caught the public imagination with their record breaking flights. The general public, however, rarely saw an aircraft unless they lived near an airfield. Here in the North it was an event to see a 'plane. If one was heard all the kids would dash out into the street and search the skies for it and talk about it for days afterwards. As a child I remember the publicity surrounding the opening of Yeadon Airport, now Leeds|Bradford Airport. A neighbour took me to see it and, to my everlasting dismay, all we saw was a field and a windsock with no sign of any 'planes! The more fortunate, and affluent, of course, might be lucky enough to visit Blackpool and, for 'five bob', have a flight round the bay. Nowadays, we can't get away from a whole variety of them which might range from a police helicopter hovering over a jammed motorway to a wide bodied jet taking 400 passengers to the Costa Brava. The first thing, then, is that it was exciting – it was new. It was a chance to do something that, under normal circumstances, one would never be able to do in a lifetime. It was a chance to 'reach for the sky.'

Many would be airmen volunteered as pilots but, with the exception of Fighter Command, other aircrew categories were equally important. We find, then, that although the hopes of thousands of would be pilots were dashed they still wanted to fly. To a large extent educational qualifications determined which of these thousands would be trained as pilots, navigators or bomb aimers – the minimum requirement being the School Certificate of Education. Wireless operators and air gunners were selected on the same basis of physical and mental fitness together with a series of aptitude tests to determine their suitability for a particular aircrew category. The majority of flight engineers came from R.A.F. ground crews – skilled fitters and mechanics who remustered to aircrew.

There was a feeling abroad in the late '30s, as the prospect of war became more imminent, that the next war would be fought in the air. As a young teenager I, for one, wasn't too sure what that entailed. True, towns and cities had been bombed in World War 1 but with nothing like the devastation of the 'Blitz' or the later air offensive on Germany. It was difficult to make comparisons with World War 1. Although my father had served throughout the war as a driver in the R.A.S.C. and had been through major campaigns such as Mons, the Somme and Ypres he would never talk about it. From one or two of his friends, however, I did glean a few facts about the sheer horror of trench warfare. One, who had been wounded on the Western Front, was taken prisoner and moved to a field medical station where one of his legs was amputated without anaesthetic. It should be stressed that the German surgeons had no alternative in those conditions and their action saved the man's life. Nevertheless, twenty years later, he regularly woke up in the middle of the night screaming and cursing from the nightmares that would never go away.

On a somewhat lighter side there was a letter from an uncle serving in the trenches. Writing to my grandmother he said: "For God's sake send me something for the lice. They are as big as fox terriers." The sequel was that grandmother sent him some ointment which had to be rubbed into the seams of his clothing. Unfortunately he didn't read the instructions and rubbed it onto his skin with disastrous results. There is no doubt that such tales influenced me and many others. One school of thought argued that if it was to be a war in the air it would be far better to be up there, bombing or strafing, than to be on the ground at the receiving end! I was also influenced by an older cousin who was training to be a fighter pilot. He sent me all his notes from Initial Training Wing (I.T.W.) where the basic theory of flight and navigation were taught so that I was well versed in the theory before I even enlisted.

In conversation with some of my Canadian colleagues I found they had similar reasons for joining aircrew. Predominant was the sense of adventure and the glamour but they seemed to have no illusions about the dangers and horrors. Doc Watson, bomb aimer in Lyn Bell's crew, writes about the stories he heard of shattered bodies being removed from aircraft and, even, of the remains of rear gunners being hosed out of their turrets. The Canadians also felt they had to follow in their fathers' footsteps and do their bit for the 'Old Country' even though most of them had never seen it before. This sentiment, of course, also applies to those who came from Australia, New Zealand, South Africa and, indeed, from every corner of the Commonwealth, or the British Empire as it was then known. Doc was particularly proud of the fact that a leading World War 1 "Ace" was the Canadian Billy Bishop, V.C.

Finally, there was that certain distinction of aircrew. On completion of training most aircrew cadets were promoted to Sergeant whilst the remainder were commissioned as Pilot Officers. More important, however, was the brevet stitched over the left breast pocket of the tunic or battledress. Whether it was the full wings of the pilot or the half wing of the navigator, bomb aimer, flight engineers, wireless operator or air gunners, it was something special and worn with pride. It was a far from easy task to earn that brevet which involved months of intensive training and intense application. Even after the passing out parade the training didn't stop. It continued through Advanced

Flying School, Operational Training, Heavy Bomber Conversion Unit and, even,a Lancaster Finishing School! Once we reached the Squadron we thought we knew it all – but we didn't! Training continued throughout our tour of operations: bombing practices for the bomb aimer, H2S cross countries flights for the navigator and fighter affiliation exercises for the gunners when Spitfires made mock attacks on the bombers and the results of successful evasion and counter attack, or otherwise, were recorded on film.

Looking back on almost five years in the R.A.F. I often wonder what I did in all that time. Of those five years I spent seven and a half months on the Squadron during which time I managed to complete a tour of ops which is what I was trained to do. Some airmen did two or, even, three tours of ops although they were in a very small minority. One reason that it took so long was the time spent hanging around in holding units waiting to proceed to the next stage of training. Three months of those five years were spent on troopships sailing to South Africa and back. Once on the Squadron the ops came thick and fast for about three months and then Robbie was promoted to Squadron Leader and made Officer Commanding "A" Flight. Flight Commanders had to spend some time in their position in order to give some stability to the Flight and a Flight Commander would often be called upon to stand in for the Squadron Commander. Hence, after December, 1944, our ops were few and far between.

I registered for service in the summer of 1940 whilst on holiday at Colwyn Bay at the age of eighteen. At that time I volunteered for aircrew as a pilot. My father had indicated his wish to see me follow in his footsteps as a driver in the R.A.S.C. When he discovered that I had volunteered as a pilot he was furious although later, of course, he relented."Well," said Ethel Broadley, daughter of the landlord of the 'Mannville Arms', our local,"you can drive a car so you should be alright as a pilot."(!) In that context it is a sobering thought that many a bomber pilot had never passed a test to drive a car!

Almost a year passed before I was officially enrolled as an A.C.2 aircrew cadet at Padgate. Here, I was interviewed at length, I.Q. tested, aptitude tested and subjected to a most searching medical. It was at Padgate that I had my first experience of eating in an airmen's mess. I, and a few other aircrew interviewees, were disdainfully picking over a plateful of stew, heavily laced with onions which I detest. "Just wait till you've been here a week," came a voice from across the aisle, "you'll eat the bloody plate!"It was at Padgate that I saw my one and only live all in wrestling match. After one bout it was announced that the winner had broken one of his opponent's legs. There was a cacophony of boos, jeers, cheers and exclamations of shock and dismay. The victim made a miraculous recovery because, the next night, he was wrestling again. After a couple of days at Padgate I was accepted for training as a pilot in the R.A.F.V.R. (Royal Air Force Volunteer Reserve) and sent back home on 'deferred service.'

Four months later, in April, 1942, I received orders to report to Stockleigh Hall in St. John's Wood, London. During those four months I had struck up a friendship with a chap called Harold who patronised our local. We discovered that we had been called up at the same time although he had to report to Viceroy Court also in St. John's Wood. There was a farewell party for us in the pub and the next day we caught the train to London – my first visit to the big city. My father had given me a £5 note – a fortune in those days – and so, feeling no rush to report, we had a few drinks in London and a meal at a Lyons Corner House. I eventually reported to Stockleigh Hall at, about, 4.30 pm. The corporal in charge was a tall, fat, harassed looking individual and I was immediately berated for being four and a half hours late. Before the war Stockleigh Hall had been a block of luxury flats and, for my billet, I had to share a tiny box room with a lad from Wales.

Memories of my six weeks in London are vague. First of all we were kitted out. We queued at the stores for a set of 'best blue', battle dress, three shirts, a tie, three sets of underwear, three pairs of socks, two pairs of boots, a forage cap with a white 'flash', a strange looking cape cum groundsheet and a housewife or 'hussif' which contained sewing materials for repairing our clothes. We also had a set of 'irons' a mug, enamel plate, webbing belt, haversack, side pack, gas mask and a kit bag. We were initiated into the art of kit inspections when we had to "stand by our beds". Kit had to be laid out in a precise manner at the foot of the bed; three blankets had to be folded in a particular manner alternated with two white sheets and the whole lot bound together with a blanket. In accounting for our linen we had to learn the formula, "One there, one on and one in the wash."

During my stay in London I learnt the rudiments of drill. There were more medicals and dental inspections and the first of a whole range of innoculations which were duly recorded on a medical card. For meals we were marched, appropriately enough, to the zoo at Regent's Park and pay parades were held at Lords Cricket Ground. After a fortnight in the R.A.F. Dad's fiver was just about gone and most of us were looking forward to our first pay – twenty eight shillings, or £1.40, for two weeks' wages! My first pay parade was a bitter disappointment. About 1,000 would be airmen were lined up on parade but the paying officer ran out of money before they reached the "W"s so, along with a hundred or so others with surnames in the 'T to Z range', I had to return the following day. Pay Parade was another ritual we had to learn. The sergeant in charge would call out: "White, A!" My response was: "Sir! 703!" I would then march smartly to the pay table, salute, collect my £1.40, salute again and march back to the ranks.

I can remember very little of the lads in "44 Intake" in London.

One who sticks in my mind was Ernie Clements who came from Birmingham. At first he seemed superior to the rest of us because he turned up in Army battledress wearing the insignia of the Home Guard whilst the rest of us were wearing 'civvies' until we had been kitted out. For some reason he attached himself to me and we were together for about six months. Jack Whitehead who came from Huddersfield was another chum and the three of us were together at Ludlow and Stratford on Avon. After three or four weeks in London we began to feel superior to the new recruits in 45 and 46 Intakes and were eager to begin training at I.T.W. (Initial Training Wing). We were often reminded that we were the cream of the R.A.F. but, as the weeks passed in routine drills, inspections and a modicum of "bull" we began to feel that the cream had gone sour. Despite the white flashes in our caps denoting our potential aircrew status we were still A.C.2s, sprogs, erks, the lowest of the low.

To be fair, it must be said that the powers that be did try to break the monotony. There were lectures and pep talks at the Rudolf Steiner Hall and sessions in aircraft recognition. There were our first Church Parades where we marched to the strains of an Air Force Band and where I was first intrigued by the order: "Fall out Roman Catholics and Jews!" It was surprising how the proportion of Roman Catholics and Jews increased as each Sunday came along! I, and a few other naive provincial lads, were also intrigued by the frequent lectures and warnings about V.D. and the dire consequences of catching a dose of one or other of its varieties. We were warned of the dangers of being allured by "enthusiastic amateurs" and advised that sex was safer with a professional prostitute although I don't think many of us could afford such services on two bob a day!. One break from routine came with a visit to a B.B.C. recording studio. It was a Ben Lyons and Bebe Daniels radio show and we were marched down to provide a live audience. I was particularly fascinated by the prompter who regularly popped on to the stage bearing a large white card which exhorted the captive audience to "CLAP", "LAUGH" or "CHEER". After three runs through of the show, however, we had had enough!

At last we received news that "the postings had come through" but it was not, alas, to I.T.W. but to Ludlow in Shropshire. Rumours abounded as to what we would do at Ludlow but the general consensus was that it was either a holding unit, where we would stay until the blockage in the training pipeline had been cleared, or it was to be a 'toughening up' course. In the event, both were right. All my memories of Ludlow are unpleasant although my own little group probably fared better than most.

R.A.F. Ludlow was nothing more or less than a huge field with a stream flowing through the middle. On one side of the stream was a large number of bell tents to which we were allocated, twelve to a tent. Kit bags, which were used as pillows, went to the tent wall and we slept with feet to the central pole. Alongside a hedge at the bottom of the field was row of latrines, perhaps twenty in all, screened off by a strip of canvas. On the other side of the stream was the field kitchen which seemed to consist of a few trestle tables, coal, or wood burning stoves and a number of enormous cauldrons. Beyond the kitchen were a few more tents for the N.C.Os. All water was taken from the stream. Upstream for drinking water and water for cooking and downstream for water for washing. 'Irons' and greasy, soot blackened cooking utensils had to be scoured until they shone by using sand from the banks of the stream.

One of the first jobs to be done at Ludlow was to construct a bridge over the stream. As trainee aircrew were selected from the so called academic elite few, if any, had any experience of manual construction work and neither had the N.C.O.s or the Pilot Officer who was in charge of our Intake. However, as I had revealed under interrogation, I had once laid some crazy paving at home and the result was that I was given responsibility for the job so our little group became bridge builders! In practice this involved laying some long, heavy railway sleepers across the stream and then covering them with a few tons of concrete. The concrete was hand mixed and the whole process took about five weeks. It was back breaking work but we enjoyed it not least because the importance of the 'bridge' saved us from a lot of the rigours and bull suffered by many of our colleagues. The summer of 1942 was one of the best of the century – in Ludlow anyway -and during that June and July we became really tanned and hardened.

There was a debit side however. There were the parades in full marching order. These entailed dressing in best blue with buttons and boots sparkling; webbing belt and cap flash blancoed whiter than white and we carried haversack, containing our full kit, gas mask, water bottle and side pack. Haversacks had to be perfectly square with no trace of a bulge which led to some lads lining their packs with cardboard. Our corporal, who was the most sadistic man I have ever met, then marched us to the 'parade ground' which was a slightly sloping part of the field. The march was accompanied by admonitions, threats, curses and dire warnings of what would happen if we batted an eyelid or put a foot wrong.

The worst part, however, was the parade itself. We would line up in flights, dress off and stand, it seemed, for hours in the hot sun. Each flight was minutely inspected by the Station Warrant Officer who was, if that is possible, worse than the corporal. It was not unusual, after standing in the sun for an hour or more, for someone to collapse from the heat or cramp but to break ranks to go to the aid of such an unfortunate would incur further penalties. Each man was inspected. 'Jankers' would be liberally dished out for the least fault-buttons less than perfect, pack not square, cap worn incorrectly, marked webbing or cap flash, hair cut, badly shaved, unpressed trousers and a score of other 'crimes'.

43

A classic example of the mentality of our corporal was illustrated when an attack of dysentery hit the camp. One night there were around a hundred of us queueing at the latrines at 1.00 or 2.00 a.m. The next day many of the men reported sick to the M.O. who dosed them up with the R.A.F's patent stomach mixture and put them on light duties for the day. Our corporal, seeing his depleted ranks, was convinced that he was being conned. After dismissing the rest of us to our tasks he rounded up the sick parade and forced them to "double" round the camp with disastrous results for those whose bowels were still loose. My only other recollection of Ludlow is the cider. When in funds and not confined to camp we would make our way to the local and drink pints of scrumpy. Beer was old hat – nothing could compare with Shropshire cider – I was immune to any ill effects until . . .

I had my first leave from Ludlow – a 48 hour pass. On arriving in Bradford I went to meet Dad at the 'Mannville'.

"What'll you have lad?" he asked.

"Oh, draught cider," I replied.

I had two pints of Tom Broadley's draught cider and was as sick as a dog for 24 hours! That was my last pint of cider!

On our return to Ludlow we were delighted to find that our real training was about to begin. We were posted to I.T.W. at Stratford on Avon. Under the new 'PNB' scheme all trainee pilots, navigators and bomb aimers undertook basic training at I.T.W. We were billeted in the 'Falcon Hotel' which was real luxury after the rigours of Ludlow. Down the street was another intake billeted in the 'Shakespeare'. Of the forty four members of my 'flight' I can remember very few names today. There was Ernie Clements and John Whitehead and my room-mate Jim ? who came from Darwen in Lancashire. I also met up with Bert Thomas who came from a little mining village in South Wales and Denis Shoebridge who had been a newspaper reporter.

It was at Stratford that we learnt the elements of flying. There were daily lectures on navigational theory where we were introduced to the mysteries of rhumb lines, great circles, map projections, courses, tracks, indicated and true airspeeds, wind velocities, triangles of velocities, E.T.A.s, drift and scores of other phenomena. There were lectures on the theory of flight, anhedral, dihedral, venturi effect, engines, instruments, compasses, meteorology, lift and drag. We practised aircraft recognition and Morse and learnt how to assemble, load and fire a Lee Enfield rifle.

In between times we had more medicals, tests for night vision, innoculations and more dental inspections. Prior to joining the R.A.F. I had a dental check up at home and was assured that my teeth were perfect. At Stratford I had twelve fillings! I am convinced that the least speck of tartar was sufficient for the dental officer to give me a filling!

Our corporals were superb. Their task was to shepherd us around to lectures and the like but also, and perhaps more important, to drill into us a sense of smartness, alertness, punctuality and pride in ourselves and in our flight. A good marching pace was 120 paces per minute. We had to do 140. We learnt precision drill so that, ultimately, 44 of us would move as one and go through the whole drill routine without one command being given. Being one of the tallest in the flight I was designated "marker". Every morning we would gather informally for parade in the street behind the "Falcon". One of the corporals would call out: "Marker!" and I had to spring to attention and march six paces into the road. At the next command the rest of the flight would fall in to my left and then, in a complicated manoeuvre to the order: "Tallest on the right, shortest on the left, in two ranks SIZE!" we would be sorted out into three ranks with the tallest at each end the shortest in the middle. We would then march off, arms swinging shoulder high, to wherever we were going.

Thursday was sports afternoon. The Ludlow summer was

I.T.W. Stratford on Avon

46

continuing and a few of us usually went boating on the River Avon. Weekends were often free although there was Church Parade on Sundays but these could sometimes be avoided. No leave was allowed until the end of the course but after a while I found a way to slip off home for the weekend returning via the milk train and a lift in a newspaper van from Birmingham which Ernie had put me wise to. I thought this was very clever of me especially as I had outwitted our corporals. I was quickly brought down to earth one Friday when Corporal Jolly called out:"Oh, White, you have a dental appointment tomorrow. You won't be able to get home will you?"

I.T.W. was one of the most formative periods of my life. The drill, discipline, studies, competition and co-operation, to name a few factors, were to prove invaluable later when I joined the Squadron. Unlike most servicemen I think most of us enjoyed the drill. For one thing, unlike Ludlow, the corporals treated us like human beings. They took pains to explain to us the purpose of this branch of our training and instilled in us a sense of pride and, even, superiority to the other intakes in training at Stratford. The end result was that we worked together like a well oiled machine and our reflexes, or reactions to commands, were honed to a split second response. Most of us passed the final examinations although poor Ernie failed and and left us to join a ground staff grade. We were given our cloth 'props' to sew on our sleeves and found ourselves promoted two ranks to L.A.C. – only one step below corporal! More important, our pay was doubled to 22.5p per day! The next step for would be pilots was Grading School. This entailed twelve hours instruction on Tiger Moths to see if one had the aptitude to be a pilot. Ideally one should solo within the twelve hours. Navigators and bomb aimers missed this stage of the training and went straight to their specialised training school. In my case, after an end of course leave, I was posted to R.A.F. Brough, near Hull.

My first instructor was a little Canadian Sergeant Pilot who insisted on giving his pupils a piece of maple sugar before a flight – probably to calm their nerves! As I climbed into the cockpit of that frail and flimsy Tiger Moth for the first time I had my first misgivings about being a pilot. I felt trapped. At I.T.W. we had studied compasses, altimeters, airspeed indicators, rudders, elevators, trim and now, there they were in front of me. How on earth could I watch all this lot and fly the thing as well? The Canadian taxied into wind and the 'plane bumped and gathered speed along the grass runway and then, for the first time in my life, I was airborne! As the earth receded below me I thought: "This is it! We'll never make it back to earth in one piece!" The pilot flew out over the Humber climbing to about 3,000 feet. Then, over the intercom, I heard:"All right buddy, it's all yours!" I gulped. "Keep her straight and level," called the little Canadian.

I clutched the stick gingerly and the nose started to come up.

"Down!" came a shout in my ears, "Keep your eyes on the horizon!

"After a while and more admonitions I began to get the hang of it and when we finally landed I was much more optimistic.

Over the next couple of weeks or so I learned to take off, climb at a steady rate, turn, bank, stall, dive and spin. I could do anything with a Tiger Moth – except land it! I was a poor judge of height and invariably put the 'plane into an attitude for a three point landing whilst twenty or thirty feet up in the air. As my instructor would dryly remark:

"Well, whadya know, no ground!"

The final humiliation came on my last lesson which was with the Chief Flying Instructor. It was he who would decree whether or not I would be a pilot. In mitigation of myself I should add that it was a wild and windy day in October when I went up for the crucial test. It is true to say that a Tiger Moth, flying into a strong wind, could be almost stationary over the airfield. The Chief Instructor, however, had decided that he could just get one more in before flying was cancelled for the day. I think I did a good cockpit drill and took off and climbed to 3|4,000 feet. The C.I. took me through the drill of turns, stalls and a spin and then, seeing that ours seemed to be the only 'plane left in the sky, decided we ought to go back. Unfortunately, in concentrating on my manoeuvres, I had lost my bearings. I remembered the cement works at Hessle and the island in the Humber but nowhere could I see the airfield.

"Take her round to starboard you fool!" bawled the C.I. Finally I found the airfield and descended to 1,000 feet. Down wind – turn left into the funnel – lower – lower – cut revs – steady – nose up – BANG! The stick was wrenched from my fingers, throttle opened wide and the C.I. took the 'plane round again and landed. And that was the end of my training as a pilot!

After a short leave I was posted to Heaton Park, Manchester, for regrading as a navigator. Heaton Park was a holding unit for trainee aircrew awaiting posting to one of the Commonwealth air training schools in Canada, South Africa or Rhodesia. It was here that I met up with Bert Thomas again, Bill Rotherham and Goff Attewell and the four of us were to be close friends for over a year. Through the winter of 1942|43 Heaton Park was the coldest, dampest and foggiest place imaginable. We sat and shivered around stoves in Nissen huts although, quite often, there was no coke to put on the stoves. An amazing number of pubs were out of bounds – probably because of the 'enthusiastic amateurs' who frequented them! We just lived for our postings to come through – for Canada we hoped.

One day in February we were marched to the stores for new kit. It was tropical kit and we were to go to South Africa. Glad as we were to be making some progress again we, nevertheless, had our misgivings about going to South Africa. After all, we now wanted to join Bomber Command and fly the new Lancasters, Halifaxes or Stirlings but we could now, possibly, land up in North Africa or the Far East for that matter. Towards the

49

end of February we embarked on a train for Blackpool. We were billeted in a boarding house in Lytham Road and had a lot of free time. There were more innoculations including a nasty one for yellow fever. Despite strict instructions to refrain from alcohol for twenty four hours one young lad from Middlesborough had a few whiskeys and passed out and, consequently, missed his posting. In fact, I received this injection on my twenty first birthday which we celebrated by going to see "Peter Pan" at a Blackpool theatre. Dad had sent me another fiver for my birthday!

One day the four of us were walking down Lytham Road and, feeling a little peckish, popped into a cafe. Food in our digs was only so so and to qualify for a cup of tea we had to wash up, clear up, clean up or dry up. Ordering rock buns and mugs of tea I commented that we didn't get much to eat in our digs. As the waitress disappeared into the back Bert remarked that she looked familiar. "She should do," muttered Bill Rotherham, "she's our bloody landlady. We'll get bugger all to eat tonight!" My only other memory of Blackpool is, again, our corporal! He was a pretty genial type but was very keen on a smart turn out and good marching. If one of us should err he would bawl out:

"Smarten up there or I'll pee in your ear!"

Early in March we boarded a train for Liverpool. With full kit, which included two kit bags, we marched to the Princess Landing Stage and, along with 4,000 others – soldiers, sailors and airmen – marched up the gangway of the "Orontes".

Chapter Four

SOUTH AFRICA

Where are the Aussies, the sports and the cobbers,
Talking of cricket and sheilas and grog;
Flying their Lancs over Hamburg and Stettin
And back to the Lincolnshire wintertime bog?

How naive can one get? An N.C.O. led us in groups of fourteen to what was known as a mess deck. Each group was divided and placed, seven at each side, at a long table.

"Oh, this must be where we eat," said I , "but I wonder where we sleep?"

"Up there, stupid!" came a voice.

"Up there" were pairs of hooks fastened into the ceiling. Somewhere, tidily stored away in lockers under the bench seats, were hammocks which were attached to a pair of hooks at night and that was where we slept! Goff, Bert, Bill and I managed to keep together on the same mess. Each day two of us would queue at the galley for the rations for our mess and a rota was devised for this and also for cleaning up.

After time allowed for sorting ourselves out we were summoned to a meeting point for lifeboat drill which was our daily muster point for the entire voyage – six weeks in all – to Durban. There was plenty of free time when we played cards or read a book if we could get hold of one. There was also a tiny canteen on board where, if we were very lucky and didn't mind queueing for hours, we could get a chocolate ration and, even, an occasional bottle of beer. The mess was inspected daily and we stood in awe of the Captain as he made his daily rounds. Every ten days or so we all had an "F.F.I." inspection which means "Free from Infection" which, I think, was mainly intended to look for signs of scabies (!?) The procedure was for us to line up on the mess deck, one behind the other, and, when in front of the M.O., drop our pants and raise our undercarriages. Needless to say, there was many a ribald comment as an airman turned away and hoisted up his pants again!

The 'Orontes' was just one of a large convoy assembled in the Mersey. One day in March, 1943, we sailed round Northern Ireland and into the Atlantic but progress was slow – perhaps eight or nine knots – as we headed west escorted by, seemingly, tiny destroyers. From the outset Goff was terribly seasick. For over a week as we edged down the Bay of Biscay he lay sick and pallid in his hammock. Bert, Bill and I would try to tempt him with a morsel of food but he would take only a mouthful of water or tea when it was available. Heartless though it may seem Goff's sickness provided a bonus for the rest of us in our mess because we could share his rations! I shall always remember the bread and butter on the Orontes – the most delicious bread and butter I have ever tasted – before or since. The ration was two slices at breakfast and supper. As we headed south and the weather became warmer Goff gradually improved and we moved our kit and blankets up on deck and slept under a lifeboat for the rest of the voyage.

Goff was a short, stocky lad with dark, curly hair. He was a farmer's son and, as a farmer, he was in a reserved occupation but it was typical of Goff that he felt he 'had to do his bit' and had volunteered for aircrew as the only way of doing it. But he deeply loved his farm and the parents he had left behind. He always carried a photograph of his Mum and Dad everywhere he went and would have a momentary look at it every night before turning in. Because of our difference in height it was Goff who christened me "Big" and "Big" I was to remain until we were all, finally, dispersed to our different squadrons.

Bert Thomas came from Ystalyfera, near Swansea, He was an inch or so taller than me though slimmer. I gathered that his family had a hard time of it during the Depression of the 'thirties' and, all the time I knew him, he saved every penny he could and remitted a substantial part of his pay home to his mother. For a long time Bert regarded the English with suspicion. Shortly after enlisting, it seems, a Londoner remarked to Bert that he thought the Welsh lived in caves. Bert, at first, took him literally but when I told him that these toffee nosed southerners held the same view of Yorkshire men he began to mellow and we became very good friends until we were eventually posted to different squadrons. Sadly, Bert was killed on his fourth or fifth op when his 'plane crashed on take off for a raid on Cologne on Christmas Eve, 1944.

Bill Rotherham was the fourth member of our quartet. He came from St. Helens, Lancashire and used to work for Pilkington's. He was a typical Lancashire lad and we had many a friendly argument about our respective 'Roses' cricket teams. During the long, six weeks voyage when we were limited to the daily rations of a troop ship he would regularly proclaim the virtues of 'lob scouse'. Although the rest of us had never heard of it and it sounded revolting I've no doubt we would have eaten buckets of it given the chance! I never really discovered what became of Bill when we returned to the U.K. although Goff had the impression that he, also, had been killed.

One other wartime friend should be mentioned – Sid Pick. Sid was much older than the rest of us, about thirty four, which was quite old for aircrew. At one time Sid had been in a cavalry regiment and, as an old soldier, was a master of 'flannel'. Prior to enlisting in the R.A.F. he had been a shopfitter and lived in

Yeadon, near Leeds. He and I trained together all the way through to Lancaster Finishing School at Hemswell. Seven weeks later he was killed on a raid on Dusseldorf.

Despite the discomfort of life on the troop ship the long six weeks voyage had its compensations. I remember seeing my first flying fish, the fluorescent wake of the ship in tropical seas, the arrival of Father Neptune as we crossed the Equator and the illicit bananas from the 'bum boats' off Freetown. One particular memory is of an evening, lying on the deck and gazing up at the mast in the clear night sky as we sailed south. On an upper deck a group of New Zealanders, who were returning home, were having a sing song and, with the gentle roll of the ship, the tip of the mast seemed to be beating time as it pointed left and right between the stars.

The convoy had split up at Gibraltar and we later heard that a number of Mediterranean bound ships had been sunk by 'U' boats. We steamed south west across the Atlantic towards Brazil and then south east again to round the Cape of Good Hope and, finally, docked at Durban. As the 'Orontes' edged towards the dockside we heard the strains of "We'll Meet Again" from somewhere down below the towering hull of the liner. Something like four thousand servicemen – soldiers, sailors and airmen - rushed to the starboard side of the ship and peered over the rail. Down below, standing on the quay side, I could see a rather plumpish lady with her head raised to the crowd of us on the main deck singing with all her heart and soul. She went through the whole Vera Lynn repertoire of those days – "White Cliffs of Dover", "When the Lights Go On Again" and the rest. After each song there were cheers from the crowded deck and a shower of coins cascaded onto the dock below. So many of us had swarmed to the starboard side of the ship that the crew had problems tieing up so the Captain ordered us all to boat stations. I later learned that this lady welcomed all the troop ships to Durban in this manner and rumour had it that she was the

Mayoress of Durban. Once the ship was properly docked little time was wasted in disembarkation and we marched to the railway siding to board a train for short journey to Clairwood.

We were greeted at Clairwood Camp, Durban, by a tough looking, suntanned sergeant with a bristly moustache and wearing natty khaki shirt and shorts which were certainly not R.A.F. issue. From the outset he made it clear that we were scum. Having said that and put the fear of God in us we didn't get much hassle at Clairwood as long as we obeyed the rules, paraded on time and looked after our billet and equipment. Our billet was a brick built 'bungalow' with a galvanised roof. The floors were concrete and, on arrival, we were given a palliasse which we were told to fill with straw. That was our bed. There were no furnishings at all. Adjacent to our billet were the ablutions with fifteen or twenty washbasins, some showers and toilets. The ablutions block, also, had a galvanised roof and one day, after the father and mother of thunderstorms, the whole place became 'live' and a few of us got a nasty shock from the static when we turned on the taps for a wash.

On the boat we had often talked of the first thing we would do when we got to Durban and all agreed, after voting down Bill Rotherham's 'lob scouse' that it should be a trip to a cafe for a big plateful of ham and eggs. For the first two or three days we were confined to camp but then we were allowed out after dire warnings about picking up coloured girls or being lured into a 'shebeen'. Every time a convoy arrived in Durban all the hotels were closed to servicemen because, it seems, six weeks confinement on a troopship usually led to a state of civil war between rival groups of soldiers, sailors and airmen. The shebeen was a sort of illicit drinking den which sold rot gut liquor. After a session at a shebeen it was the rule, rather than the exception, to find oneself lying in the street in the early hours of the morning not just simply robbed but completely stripped as well! Goff, Bill, Bert and I found our cafe. It was a small Greek establishment with the dining area divided by a lattice screen. We had just relished and finished our meal when we heard a commotion at the other side of the screen and, seconds later, a British 'Tommy' flew backwards through the screen with a ferocious matelot falling on top of him. Needless to say, the four of us beat a hasty retreat!

Duties at Clairwood were light. The four of us were delegated to sort mail at the camp post office which was a pleasant enough job and, of course, we always got our 'airgraph' mail promptly. Most afternoons would find us at one of the delightful beaches around Durban such as Isipingo or Amamzimtoti which were our favourites although one had to be on the look out for sharks. Durban abounded with organisations which provided good, reasonably priced meals for servicemen and, after a day on the beach, we would go to the Jewish Club, Church Army, Y.M.C.A. or any of half a dozen others where we could get an appetising meal for one shilling (5p)! Food at the camp was also quite good but we could never decide what kind of meat was served up. It was usually roast and tasted rather like pork although it was much darker in colour and the wags were adamant that it was either vildebeest, hippo, rhino or wild boar! 'Tiffin' or tea usually consisted of liberal helpings of bread, butter and cheese.

It was at Clairwood that we had our first contact with apartheid. We were dismayed to learn that a young Bantu who came to collect our laundry each week was a University graduate but laundrying was all the work he could get. We were similarly affected by segregation in park benches, swimming pools, railway carriages and the rest. On one occasion I noticed two joiners working in a building, one was white, the other black. I discovered that the white joiner was paid £8 per week whilst his partner received only £1.50. Whatever our feelings may have been about these injustices we were regularly warned to keep

Standing: 4th from left – Bill Rotherham   4th from right – Bert Thomas   Sitting: 3rd from right – Goff Attewell

our mouths shut and not to get involved with the politics of the country.

One evening, after an afternoon on the beach at Isipingo, I discovered I had developed a rash. I was also feeling a bit groggy and light headed and put it down to an overdose of sun. The next morning, however, Bill shook me and bawled:

"My God! What's happened to your face?" I looked in a mirror and found myself covered with a bright red rash. In fact it seemed to cover my whole body. Without further ado I was hounded off to the sick bay and was treated like a pariah! As I walked between the rows of bungalows towards the sick quarters dozens of airmen sprang back like the waters of the Red Sea to get as far away from me as possible. The M.O. immediately diagnosed German Measles! I had to take every scrap of kit, including the palliasse, to be fumigated and I was then whipped off in an ambulance to an isolation hospital. It didn't add to my popularity either when the rest of the lads in our billet had to have their kit fumigated as well! However, the next ten days were idyllic. I slept in a real bed with real sheets in a cool, airy ward attended by beautiful South African nurses. Each day the Red Cross would come round with books, chocolates, magazines and other luxuries. My main worry was that I would miss my posting and thus be separated from my pals. Fortunately, this didn't happen because two days after returning to Clairwood we were all posted together to East London to recommence our navigation training at No. 48 Air School. Over seven months had elapsed since I had left Grading School at Brough. On the 11th June, 1943, we began an intensive course of air navigation which lasted for nine weeks.

Memories of East London are vague. Discipline was easy but the work and studies were demanding and concentrated.

Having first told us to forget everything we had learned at I.T.W. we were plunged into hours of D.R. (Dead Reckoning) navigation plotting imaginary flights all over South Africa and the Southern Hemisphere. Early on in the course the lecturer came to see how I was getting on with the plotting exercise I was working on and noted a clear black track I had carefully measured on the chart."What kind of pencil are you using?" he asked. I showed him my nicely sharpened HB."Do you realise," he said, "that on a chart of the scale you are using that track would be about two miles wide?"It was a very important point. With courses and wind velocities plotted in a similar manner the error could be compounded to several miles. Ever after that I always made sure I had a good stock of 3H pencils.

It was at East London that we were introduced to the art of astro-navigation. We memorised the constellations of both hemispheres although, of course, we couldn't see Polaris and other stars of the Northern Hemisphere. There was a quota of sextant shots to reach – hundreds of them – by day and night and the results laboriously calculated and plotted as position lines on charts. Photography, gunnery,instruments, meteorology, radio and aircraft recognition filled in the hours not spent on navigation. We practised sending and receiving Morse until we were accurate at eight words per minute. Much of our spare time was spent practising with the sextant or studying the manual of Air Navigation learning new ways of determining wind velocities, planning interceptions or making a square search. At the end of the course we would be examined on everything we had studied. Hence, there was little time for leisure – except on Thursdays, or 'shopping day'.

In charge of us was a little sergeant who was as good natured as a sergeant could be. Unfortunately, he had a very monkey like face! After lunch on Thursdays he would march us down to East London and always took us to the zoo where we were dismissed outside the monkey cage! Rumour had it that he was a bit thick because he used to say some surprising things. One story tells of the Commanding Officer ordering the sergeant to make sure there was a 100% attendance at parade the following day.

"You can't have 100% parade Sir," allegedly replied the sergeant, "there's only eighty eight men on the unit."

On Thursdays, then, we would do our shopping, have a meal and, maybe go to the cinema or the 'bioscope' as the South Africans called it.

At the end of the course I passed as 'Above Average' with a course mark of 71%. After all the delays of the past year or so things now started to speed up. Within a week we had made the two days train journey to Queenstown, high up on the South African Veldt. Almost immediately we began our course of actual flying training on the twin engined Anson. Queenstown was a market town lying in the foothills of the Drakensburg Mountains. Just a few miles away was "Hangklip", a distinctively slab shaped mountain, affectionately named "Old Faithful" by budding navigators, which was an invaluable aid when trying to find our way home back to base.

For flying exercises we were sent up in pairs – first and second navigator – and took it in turns to plot, map read, take drift readings and wind up the Anson's undercarriage! I was usually paired with either Bert or a Corporal Bill Williams. Bill had been in the R.A.F. Police but had remustered to aircrew. Navigation instruction was under the direction of Flight Lieutenant Gordon, a true Scot and former mariner. He was more than an instructor to us – more like a father who took a personal interest in the progress of each one of us. At the same time he made us work and regularly checked that we were keeping up with our quota of astro shots both on the ground and in the air. Ground training continued much as before but now we put theory into practice by flying a large number of navigational exercises over the Transkei, Eastern Cape and, occasionally, to the coast at Grahamstown or Port Elizabeth.

Our pilots were all members of the South African Air Force and most of them had done a tour of operations in North Africa. They must have been bored to tears by flying "sprog" navigators around for three or four hours at a time. One or two of them would take a book to read when "George", the automatic pilot, was in operation whilst another regularly read the Bible. Navigating by day in South Africa was fairly easy. Towns were few and far between and, in the clear South African skies, could be seen miles away. It wasn't unknown for pilots to fly so low over a railway station that the navigator could read the name! When not flying or at lectures we would do extra navigational training in a sort of navigational Link Trainer. This entailed sitting at a navigation table, complete with plotting chart and maps, and looking at a small cinema screen which simulated a flight. Through the headphones could be heard the roar of aircraft engines and the instructions and admonitions of the instructor as the 'flight' proceeded across country. The big snag was that the whole exercise was geared to a metronomic clock which made an hour 'pass' in about forty minutes. The whole idea was to have us navigating under stress and to speed up reactions so that we would be that much better prepared for the real thing.

Night flying was another matter. For this we were posted to Aliwal North, a Spa town, about 120 miles north on the Orange River. Aliwal was famous for its 'radio springs', three pools rich in minerals, heated by hot gaseous bubbles rising from beneath the earth. The temperature of the water ranged from 98.4 degrees in the smallest pool to 75.5 degrees in the largest where we went for a swim every day. During the fortnight or so we spent at Aliwal I only managed about four hours flying. We had arrived at Aliwal at the beginning of the thunderstorm season. Regularly, at 4.00p.m. each day, cumulonimbus clouds would build up and thunderstorms would lash the town for two or three hours. By nightfall the skies were clear but, quite often, electrical storms would continue making radio navigation very difficult if not impossible. Nor did it help matters for me, on one occasion, when an instructor, flying as second navigator, spent all his time chatting to the pilot instead of assisting me with the map reading. We returned to Queenstown for another fortnight's day flying followed by a week of examinations.

Although the work load was heavy we did have some time for relaxation. The citizens of Queenstown had developed a scheme whereby families would 'adopt' an airman for his stay at Queenstown. Goff and Bill were not keen on this idea but Bert and I decided to have a go. The outcome was that, one Friday, a South African trader and his wife picked us up at camp in their 'Oldsmobile'. These were the Jeffreys and they had a trading post at a little settlement called Kamastone about twenty miles away. With them was their sixteen year old daughter, Daphne, and a niece, Dorothy. The girls were away at a boarding school during the week but returned home at weekends. Sometimes the Jeffreys would take us into town for dinner and, maybe, a film show before proceeding home.

They lived in a massive bungalow up on the Veldt with its own electricity and water supply. It was staffed by Bantu women who did all the cooking and cleaning whilst their menfolk worked on the land adjoining the bungalow. The trading post was like a Wild West general store and seemed to sell everything. Mr. Jeffreys would buy maize and other produce from the natives and sell them the goods they needed from his store. Close to the bungalow was a tennis court where we would all have a game or two on Saturdays or Sundays. Both Mr. and Mrs. Jeffreys were well in their 50s and were well endowed, weighing around 200 pounds each but, nevertheless, they could both chase Bert and me around the tennis court.

It was customary, after dinner, to play a few hands of a version of 'Rummy' which used three or four packs of cards and after this Bert and I and the girls were instructed to "go outside and count the stars." Although it is hard to believe, Bert and I, being five or six years older than the girls, never considered making a pass and, believe it or not, we went walks to the Methodist Mission where we would often listen to the Negro choir or join

'Hangklip' nr. Queenstown.

the minister and his family for a social evening. Later, we would return to have a night cap of South African 'Commando' brandy with Mr. Jeffreys. They were a wonderful family and I often wonder what became of them.

On the 1st December, 1943, we learnt that we had successfully completed the course. The following day our "Wings Dinner" was held at the Windsor Hotel in Queenstown and I still have Goff's menu with all our autographs decorating it. On the front is inscribed: "L.A.C. Attewell – nearly Sergeant!" Friday, the 3rd, was taken up with packing, sewing on our sergeant's stripes and the press studs for our navigator's brevet which would be clipped on by the Commanding Officer at the Wings Parade which was held on Saturday, 4th December. The C.O. congratulated us and shook hands with us in turn as he attached our brevets to the press studs. I doubt if there was a man amongst us who did not cast a surreptitious glance down to his top, left hand pocket to admire the half wing with its embroidered "N" which we had strived so long and hard for. The Jeffreys came along to the Wings Parade and congratulated Bert and I but within minutes of the end of the parade we were embarking in lorries for the railway station. The Jeffreys followed us to the station and Daphne gave me a farewell present of a leather cigarette case. Then it was, "All aboard!" and we were off.

During our stay in South Africa the war had seemed a long way off and we had almost forgotten the rationing, restrictions, black out and deprivations of wartime Britain. Of course, the main news came through and we already had a vague idea of the new, 'magic' "Gee" which was now in service with Bomber Command. Gee was a navigational device that could pinpoint one's position within half a mile and was fitted to all the new four engined heavy bombers for the air offensive against Germany. Whilst we were training, 6,000 miles away, this offensive had built up and, by the time we were getting our wings, the Battles of the Ruhr and Berlin were well under way.

We heard that losses were heavy though "sustainable" which meant, in effect, that the average crew might complete twenty 'ops' – ten short of a full tour. Now, we were almost trained to help replenish the squadrons.

Not all of us, however, were to return to the U.K. Sadly, Goff and six or seven others were posted to the Middle East to join the Desert Air Force. Still, we were to have another month together so we made the most of it. After another two days train journey back to Durban we arrived at Clairwood again and were greeted by the same, bristly moustached sergeant but now, of course, we were also sergeants! We were Sergeant Navigators which was more important and our pay was now £4.30 per week!

His first words, in clipped tones, as he lined us up were:

"Well, gentlemen, the last time I saw you you were L.A.C.s. Now you are sergeants, the same as me. Let me tell you now that, as far as I am concerned, you are still bloody L.A.C.s!" And so we were!

This time our stay in Durban was short – about a fortnight. With our new wealth we bought presents to take home to our families in rationed England. Amongst other items I had two bottles of South African Commando Brandy and Advokaat in my kit bag. A week or so before Christmas we embarked on the S.S. Pulaski, a Polish freighter of about 7,000 tons. The accommodation was even worse than that on our outward voyage but we quickly organised ourselves some pitches under the lifeboats again. It was now terribly hot in the Southern Hemisphere summer and it was a relief to sail out of harbour into the Indian Ocean. Accompanying us was another freighter, the "City of London" and, escorted by a single destroyer, we headed north at eight knots.

Day after day for almost three weeks City of London and Pulaski plodded over 3,000 miles to Aden. The escort left us off Mombasa and from then on we sailed alone. The sea was calm and Goff suffered no further bouts of sickness. Over forty years

20 New Navs. (Queenstown)

later, at our little reunion in Usk, I discovered that Goff must have had some undetected stomach problem because he suffered severely when flying with the Desert Air Force and was ultimately forced to take a ground posting with flying control. He had never complained of his disability and it was only discovered by accident when he passed out on an operation half way through his tour.

The days passed slowly – reading, playing cards or just lazing on deck. For Christmas dinner we had tinned turkey but it could have been anything. We anchored at Aden where 'Pulaski' was refuelled. For hours a steady procession of Arabs dumped sacks of coal down chutes into the bunkers. That night we turned in as usual around 10.00p.m. We were awakened by a most unholy row – it seemed as though every ship in the harbour was sounding its fog horn.

"Had "U" boats been sighted?" "Was the war over?"

The noise continued and, gradually, a pattern could be distinguished:

". . ... .- .—. .—. – .— -. . .— -.— . .- .-. etc." It was "Happy New Year from the City of London." and the reply "Happy New Year from Pulaski." sent out in Morse on fog horns for all Aden to hear! We had lost track of time – it was New Year's Day, 1944. I rooted in my kit bag and extracted the brandy and advokaat and poured it into our enamel mugs thus heralding in 1944!

The following day we again set sail up the Red Sea and finally disembarked at Port Taufiq. Although we stayed here for only a few days memories are vivid. The Navy had set up a row of trestle tables and we were given half a loaf of bread, a lump of some kind of margarine which, even in the desert heat, was as solid as a rock and seemed to crumble into the bread, a large dollop of jam and a mug of tea. Once again, home was a bell tent but, instead of the lush meadows of Ludlow the floor was sand and the tent was a haze of flies.

Toilet facilities were primitive. Urinals were big funnels stuck into the sand. The latrines consisted of a long wooden bench, with suitable holes in it about eighteen inches apart, arranged over a seemingly bottomless pit. One would sit over the selected hole grimly grasping the board with both hands which was no mean feat as one was constantly dive bombed by flies as big as sparrows! Wherever one walked on the camp there would be an Arab in attendance trying to sell some leather work or some other souvenir of Taufiq. The farther one walked, the lower would fall the price. To visit the camp cinema was an experience to remember. This was an enormous tin shack with benches on the sandy floor. For most performances it would be packed but the hundreds of pairs of feet would stir up the sand so that a permanent cloud of dust obscured the screen and, of course, there were the flies.

It was at Taufiq that I met battle hardened soldiers for the first time – "Desert Rats" from Montgomery's 8th Army, Commandos and Paratroopers. Here, also, Goff and I made our sad farewells as, with a wistful grin, he said:"So long, Big. I reckon we'll meet up again someday in the U.K." With that, we were lined up in our respective drafts to go to our respective postings. A feature of the shacks and buildings around the camp and dock side was the inscription "R.O.T.B." – Roll On The Boat! It was a simple enough sign expressing the yearning of thousands of servicemen to get back home. I thought of Goff and his beloved farm and pictured him taking his nightly look at the photograph in his wallet. By coincidence we were marched aboard the 'Orontes' again. After three weeks on the 'Pulaski' the 'Orontes' was like a luxury liner and, so, we set sail for home. The African campaign was over and the Mediterranean was clear for our shipping. As we left the "Med." we packed away our tropical kit and, once again, wore our 'blues'.

On a cold, wet night. towards the end of January, we disembarked at Liverpool where my first recollection is of the

"Sally Ann" dishing out mugs of hot tea and beans on toast. We entrained for, of all places, Harrogate where we were billeted in the 'Majestic Hotel'. Two days later I caught the bus home along with a W.A.A.F. who was the daughter of one of Dad's Mannville pals, Billy Dinsdale. Within an hour we were both in the local having a pint.

Chapter Five

TOWARDS THE SQUADRON

Where are the fliers from Canada's prairies,
From cities and forests determined to win,
Thumbing their noses at Hitler's Luftwaffe
And busily dropping their bombs on Berlin.

Following disembarkation leave and a week or so in Harrogate it looked as though the training pipeline was blocked again for we were posted to Whitley Bay for a "toughening up" course. At 6.30 a.m. in the bitter February cold we were put through our paces on the sands or drilled and marched along the sea front. After the sun of the tropics and the desert this was one way of getting us acclimatised again to the British climate. Fortunately, our stay in Whitley Bay wasn't too long – about three weeks – and we assembled once again for our posting to Advanced Flying School at West Freugh in Scotland.

The purpose of No. 4 Advanced Flying School was to get us accustomed to flying around Britain which was a tremendous change to flying around the wide open spaces of South Africa. The climate also provided a big change flying, as we did, over cloud for much of the time whereas our earlier training had taken place in almost cloudless skies. Navigating in Ansons we learned how to put more reliance on W|T for our bearings and fixes. Map reading also involved the identification of light houses and a new language of flashing and occulting beams. The navigational exercises, of about three hours duration, took us up and down the west coast, Irish Sea, Isle of Man, Anglesey and South West Scotland. On one occasion, during a night exercise, the radio broke down and we had to land at Mona in Anglesey. We spent the night there and returned to base the following day. There was more practice firing from gun turrets, more aircraft recognition and more Morse practice. After three weeks at West Freugh our training seemed to end abruptly because we were quickly posted to No. 18 Operational Training Unit at Finningley, near Doncaster. It had taken me about two years to reach this stage which was the penultimate stage of training before joining squadrons for the real thing.

Now, for the first time, there seemed to be a sense of urgency about our training. For one thing, most of the instructors had done a tour of ops and we were learning from men who had first hand experience of the problems and dangers that we would be up against. Throughout May we had hours of plotting in the navigation section but now we were using charts of North West Europe which marked the towns and cities we would be attacking in the near future. There were more lectures on Met., Instruments, Aircraft Recognition, Parachutes, Air Sea Rescue and a host of other topics. For the first time we were taught the techniques of Pathfinders learning about target indicators, "Wanganui", "Window" and the magic box "Gee".

Gee was a radar device which picked up pulses from transmitters in England. These pulses appeared on a circular screen as 'blips' which moved across the screen on two lines, or time bases. With the aid of various knobs and switches pairs of blips could be aligned on the screen and a reading could then be obtained which was plotted on a special chart. By very careful tuning of the blips and precise timing Gee provided a position fix far more accurate than any other type of fix except an actual 'pinpoint' of the ground obtained visually. As such pinpoints, in practice, were few and far between Gee was an invaluable aid to accurate navigation. The only problem was that its range was reduced by enemy jamming by the time we began to use it. The jamming produced zig zag lines over the screen, green fuzz and 'false' blips.

I spent many hours of my spare time in the "Gee Room" practising and trying to separate the blips from the artificial interference made by the trainer. Similarly I spent a lot of time plotting my readings on the charts, carefully interpolating between the printed position lines and gradually building up my speed. We were trained to obtain a Gee fix every six minutes. The distance between two fixes would be measured on the chart and the ground speed quickly calculated by multiplying the distance between the fixes by ten. It was then a fairly simple matter to estimate the aircraft's position six minutes ahead and calculate a new course and E.T.A. (Estimated Time of Arrival) at the turning point or destination.

For four or five weeks navigators underwent intensive training during which time two main themes were stressed: keeping exactly on track and exactly on time. Meanwhile an assortment of pilots were undergoing their own training and learning all there was to learn about the Wellington bomber – the old and much loved 'Wimpey'- once the mainstay of Bomber Command. Similarly, bomb aimers were receiving their own specialised training on bomb sights, PFF markers, flares, photography, map reading, 'window' and, of course, the huge variety of bombs and fuses they would be dealing with on a squadron. Wireless operators and air gunners were dispersed to other units for their training and it wasn't until early June that all branches of aircrew could be seen wandering around the huge hangars at Finningley. The time had come to be "crewed up".

By this time most of my South African pals had been posted to other units but Bert Thomas and Sid Pick remained with me. Another "elderly" navigator, aged thirty four, had joined us. He was Bill Grimshaw who came from Sale, Manchester, and he later went on to be an instructor. On crewing up day the navigators had been told to remain in the navigation section and to see what happened! After a while a pilot would pop his head in the doorway and ask if "so and so" was there. "So and so" was then asked if he would care to be the navigator and then they would go off to collect the rest of the crew. Sitting by the window on this lovely summer's day I watched a steady procession of pilots and navigators depart for the hangar or the gunnery and wireless sections until only Sid, Bill and I remained. Suddenly Bill exclaimed:

"Look, Big, here's a smasher for you!"

Striding, in a determined manner, towards the doorway was a stocky, Canadian Flight Lieutenant wearing the red and white ribbon of the Air Force Cross. Sure enough, a head popped round the doorway and, in a brisk North American twang, asked:

"Hey, is one of you fellers Sergeant White?"

To a mere sergeant a Flight Lieutenant was only two steps down from God and in some awe I answered:

"Yes, that's me." or words to that effect."

Howdy," said he, "I'm Dave Robb. How'dya like to be my navigator?"

"Fine," said I gazing in awe at his A.F.C.

He led me to another Canadian, a tall, weather beaten Flying Officer, wearing a battered flat dress cap and a bomb aimer's brevet.

"Meet Ernie Mosure, or Mo, our bomb aimer." said the Flight Looey. "Mo, this is Art White our navigator."

"Howdy," said Mo,"I'm sure glad to meet you."

We went off together to find the rest of the crew and chatted, briefly, about our backgrounds and pre war careers. Mo had worked in the timber industry in British Columbia and seemed to have worked in all branches from lumberjack to running a saw mill. Our new skipper, "Call me Robbie," had been employed in some type of administration in wheat marketing in Winnipeg but he had enlisted early on in the war and had several thousand hours as an instructor in his log book.

We met up with the rest of the crew in the hangar. Chatting together in a corner were three young sergeants. The first was Ronnie Brown who was to be our wireless operator. Ronnie had worked as a clerk at a coal mine in Chester le Street, Co. Durham and joined the R.A.F. as a wireless operator|airgunner. The other two wore the Canadian shoulder flash on their tunics and they were our air gunners. Bob Gibson, or Gibby as he was called, was a slim, lithe teenager from Innisfail, Alberta. After leaving school he had worked for a short time on a farm and, at the age of seventeen and a few months, had enlisted in the R.C.A.F. Completing the crew was Monty, Charles Montague Kerr, who had also joined up at the earliest opportunity against a lot of opposition from his father who, no doubt, thought that he was a bit too young , at seventeen, to be going off fighting a war. This method of crewing up was probably the most haphazard thing the R.A.F. did. The method seemed to vary from O.T.U. to O.T.U. One method was to send everybody to a hangar and tell them to sort themselves out into crews. I gather that Monty and Gibby paired themselves off first of all and then offered their joint services to Robbie – Gibby having decided that he would be "tail end Charlie", the rear gunner. I'm not too sure why Robbie chose me in particular as his navigator but, at the time, he told me he wanted an Englishman who had trained in South Africa. The "Daddy" of the crew was Mo who was thirty five which was old for aircrew but, I gather, Mo had excelled in his training and had been granted a commission. Robbie was twenty six, Ronnie nineteen and the gunners barely eighteen whilst I was twenty two.

We now had to train together as a crew so that, ultimately, we would all work together like parts of a well oiled machine. We were posted to Gamston, near Worksop, for our operational flying training where we flew Wellingtons. After the Anson the 'Wimpie' seemed enormous but even that was to be surpassed by the Halifax and Lancaster. On the ground we learned more about our future 'cargoes' of 4,000lb. 'cookies', incendiaries, high explosives, armour piercing bombs, 'window' and photo flares. We practiced parachute drill, dinghy drill and ditching drill and we had to know the Wimpie inside out. We had our own particular responsibilities apart from our flying trade such as the removal of hatches in an emergency, releasing the dinghy, care of the Verey pistol, oxygen cylinders, fire axe, destructive charges and a score of other items.

We first flew together as a crew on "D" Day, 6th June, 1944. The flight consisted of a few "circuits and bumps" for Robbie's benefit and a short cross country for the rest of us for familiarisation and air experience in the Wellington. Then, every other day, the flights became longer building up to six hour cross countries which usually included a bombing exercise for Mo. After our usual three hour stints in the Anson six hours seemed a long time in the air but, as we would find out later, we would be having even longer trips than those. Towards the end of June we began to convert to night flying and after about ten hours of circuits and bumps the instructors decided that Robbie "would do" and we proceeded to further training on night cross countries. Again, the length of the exercises increased up to five or six hours. The cross countries ended with a bombing practice for Mo and an occasional visit to a demonstration of target indicators. From the outset Mo took his job seriously, as, indeed. we all did. He was a first class bomb aimer and nearly always got full marks for his bombing exercises. There were air to air firing and fighter affiliation exercises for Monty and Gibby and they developed a system of systematically searching the skies for other aircraft. When not working at his radio, sending or receiving messages, Ronnie also would take his turn in the astro dome as an extra look-out. Meanwhile, I speeded up on my Gee and practised "homing" the 'plane along a position line to bring the 'plane spot on to the bombing range or over the airfield. On our first night exercise we were flying with a pilot instructor who had completed his tour of ops and was, probably, a bit jumpy, at flying with a "sprog" crew. Somewhere near Fishguard we received radio instructions to return to base as bad weather was closing in. The instructor immediately asked me for a course for base.

"Hang on a minute." I replied.

"I want it NOW navigator!" snapped the instructor, "We can't wait!"

Now this sort of order wasn't in the book. Navigation was done by a pre-arranged flight plan constantly amended by changes in circumstances as they arose such as changes in wind velocity. To plot out a new course required a few minutes to draw in a new track from an estimated position a few minutes ahead, calculation of the course after taking into account winds, magnetic variation, compass deviation and E.T.A. Under this new pressure I looked at my chart and visualised a line from Fishguard to Worksop and made a blind guess.

"Navigator to Skipper, alter course 045 degrees compass."

"045 degrees." came the reply.

Hoping this would keep the instructor quiet for a few minutes I worked out the new course and gave him the E.T.A. In the event, only one other, minor alteration of course was needed and, with the aid of Gee, I homed the Wimpie right over base. When we landed and taxied back to the dispersal I overheard the instructor speaking to Robbie:

"That's a good nav you've got there Robbie."

Little did he know!

Our last cross country exercise from Worksop took us the nearest we had been, so far, to a real op. Main force bombers were out attacking the Ruhr and we formed part of a diversionary force sent out over the North Sea to a point just off the Dutch coast where we threw out a load of window to fox the German defences and then flew home again. The whole trip was uneventful.

It was generally accepted that rank was non existent in aircrew. The pilot was captain, irrespective of rank, so a Sergeant Pilot could have a Flight lieutenant as his navigator, for example. Maybe some of us took this a bit too literally because Robbie was determined to have a first class crew and felt it was his duty to lick us all into shape. One day Ronnie led a 'deputation' of Gibby and Monty to me although, like them, I was only a sergeant."Art," said he,"can you do anything about Robbie? He's bull shitting Monty, Gibby and I around something awful!"Apparently one or two of them had received a ticking off for some minor detail of untidiness such as an incorrectly worn cap or poorly polished shoes. Robbie had a Canadian pal, Flight Lieutenant Art Green, A.F.C. ,who also gave the impression of being a bit of a stickler and I guessed there was a bit of rivalry between the two of them. Diffidently I approached Robbie about it pointing out that it was't a good thing to be having any aggro in the crew."O.K. Art," he replied, "let's forget it. We'll all go down to the pub tonight." And that was the only disagreement we ever had.

On one training flight Robbie, sitting up front flying the kite, made repeated checks with individual members of the crew to see that everything was O.K. "Skipper to rear gunner. How she go there Gibby?" and similarly to the rest of us. For some reason it was Ronnie who got the most attention. Working away at his radio he was constantly interrupted by Robbie asking him for one thing or another. Finally, we heard a very exasperated Ronnie on the intercom:

"Wireless operator to Skipper."

"Yes." answered Robbie.

"Hey, Skipper, will you pass me the brush?"

"What brush?" queried Robbie.

"The brush to stick up my arse so that I can sweep the kite out whilst I am doing all these other jobs you want seeing to!"

One other experience at Worksop is worth recording. We had often been warned of oxygen lack when flying at high altitudes. In practice we used oxygen at heights over 8,000 feet but, until we arrived at O.T.U. we had never been anywhere near that height. Here, however, we regularly flew between 10,000 and 15,000 feet. Attached to our face mask which housed the intercom mike was a flexible rubber tube which we attached to an oxygen point at our flight position. The co-pilot, or flight engineer, would turn on the main supply which supplied oxygen to all positions. Should a crew member wish to leave his position he would disconnect his supply and use one of the portable oxygen bottles which held about ten minute's supply. Shortage of oxygen at high altitudes led to all sorts of conditions – even death. The most obvious symptons, to the observer, were loss of faculties, slurring of speech, false confidence or, in short, the attitude and mannerisms of a very drunk man.

One day our crew was detailed for a decompression test. We sat in a large steel chamber and attached our oxygen tubes to the appropriate supply point. The supply at one of these points had been turned off although no-one knew which point was affected. Gradually the air pressure in the chamber was reduced to simulate increasing altitude. Over the intercom the officer in charge of the test asked various members of the crew questions regarding their competence to carry out their duties. In my case I was asked if I felt alright, could I still work out a course and so on. To all the questions I replied a confident, "Yes Sir."

Gradually the altimeter climbed to about 25,000 feet when the test ended.

"Now navigator," came the officer's voice, are you sure you could plot courses?"

"Quite sure." I replied.

"Did you play cards during the test?"

"No Sir!" said I, thinking what a stupid question that was.

"Show him, Skipper." said the voice.

Robbie pointed to the area around me. Strewn around the seat and the floor were dozens of playing cards!

"Did you write your name? came the voice again.

Again I replied,"No Sir."

"Are you absolutely certain?"

"Yes, I'm certain I didn't write my name."

Robbie handed me two or three sheets of paper with my name scrawled all over them. Of course, I had been the guinea pig but it had been a salutary experience not only for me but for the rest of the crew also.

After two months of intensive training we completed the course at Finningley at the beginning of July when we were granted a week's well earned leave when I planned to get married! I had met Freda, who came from Brooklands in Cheshire, on a day trip to Blackpool in 1941. We had corresponded and visited each other at our respective homes in Bingley and Brooklands until I enlisted in the R.A.F. Although we still corresponded we didn't see each other very often until I was posted to Heaton Park and, just as it seemed we had managed to pick up the threads again, I was posted to South Africa. However, we managed to keep in touch and my few short leaves on return to the U.K. were divided between Freda and my folks in Bingley. Nobody thought marriage was a good idea for a member of an aircrew in wartime – it left a lot of widows. However, we decided to press ahead and were married in Sale as soon as I got home on leave. Our honeymoon was a few short days in Blackpool following which I had to report, with the rest of the crew, to Lindholme.

Lindholme was a heavy bomber conversion unit where we did a four weeks course on the four engined Halifax heavy bomber. It was here that we picked up the seventh member of our crew,our flight engineer, Arthur Gamble, who, as mentioned above was promptly re-christened "Poker" by Mo. To the rest of us he already looked a seasoned veteran as he was wearing the ribbon of the 1939/43 Star. He had enlisted in 1940 as a fitter and, after training, had been shipped out to the Far East. He had some hair raising tales to tell of the Japanese onslaught on Singapore and he was very lucky to escape via Java and Ceylon which is a story in itself. He eventually returned to the U.K. and remustered as a flight engineer. As at O.T.U. crewing up was a haphazard affair. He tells how the Engineering Officer, Flight Lieutenant Knight, assembled the engineers in a hangar. He was holding a list of pilots in his hand and, addressing his expectant audience said:

"I have a list of pilots here ranging from Flight Looeys down to sergeants. Now I'm going to read each one out and if you fancy him just give me a shout. O.K.?" Then he went on:

"First I have a Canadian Flight Looey with an A.F.C., name of Robb. Who wants him?"

After a couple of seconds Arthur gave him a shout:

"I'll have him!" Vin took his name and number and said:

"O.K. go into the hangar and make yourself known. You'll find them all in there waiting to see what they've got!"

And so it came about. Arthur soon found us and Robbie quickly introduced him to the rest of us. "But ... Oh Gee!" said Robbie, "we can't have two Arts in the crew. Whadya think Mo?"

"Goddam right," growled Mo, "we'll have to call him Poker!"

For my part I was particularly pleased to have a fellow Yorkshireman join us in the crew and our friendship is as strong as ever after 50 years.

At Lindholme Navigators were introduced to another 'magic box' known as "H2S" or "Y". This was another radar device which sent pulses down to the ground which were 'bounced back' and picked up by a receiver. The signals appeared on a screen, known as a plan position indicator, with varying degrees of intensity. Water didn't return a signal so a coastline, river or lake would show up black against a greyish tinge for countryside and bright areas of light for towns. The centre of the screen represented the aircraft and the aircraft's position could be ascertained by taking a bearing and range from a ground feature appearing on the screen. In short, the navigator got a radar map of the ground and, with the aid of special charts, towns could be identified by their shape provided that the navigator "read" the screen and chart as he would in normal map reading. Unfortunately, H2S signals could be picked up by the enemy so its use was prohibited until the bomber force was well over Germany.

Again, at Lindholme, we practised the various crew drills and got to know the Halifax. There were more navigational cross countries where H2S was practised intensively and we did another two diversionary flights to the Dutch coast whilst main force was out bombing targets inside Germany. Poker took an intense interest in the work of the rest of us. As flight engineer most of his work involved helping and advising Robbie where his knowledge of the aircraft and engines was invaluable. We all turned to him for advice on such things as the hydraulic system and generators where these mysteries affected our own particular job. He recalls our first night cross country, which included a diversion, where we flew for six hours above cloud.

"Navigator to Skipper, you can descend now, we should be over base."

We broke cloud at 3,000 feet and Poker was amazed to see the Lindholme runway lights directly below. The following day I enlightened him by illustrating the wonders of Gee!

At the end of four weeks we were putting the finishing touches to our training and looking forward to another week's leave. It so happened that Poker was going to do what I had done at the end of O.T.U – get married! Like me, he had encountered the same objections to such a step but he and Annie went ahead and tied the knot as soon as he got home.

As most of the remainder of this narrative is given from the navigator's point of view it might be useful at this stage to describe the factors involved in a successful bombing operation. The first requirement was, obviously, to find the target. Even with cloudless skies and a 'bombers' moon' this was not always easy. Most of the time the route to the target and, even, the target itself would be obscured by cloud; German decoy fires could lead the bombers away from the true target and a flight plan course could be quickly wrecked by adverse winds, mechanical problems or enemy action. Hence, accurate navigation was essential. Secondly, the attack itself had to be concentrated into as short a time as possible so that the enemy defences, such as fire services and anti aircraft defences, could be swamped. Ideally, then, forces of, up to, 1,000 bombers should be over the target in the space of twenty to thirty minutes. To achieve this each squadron would be given a precise altitude to fly and a precise time to bomb. If we were told to bomb at 0112 hrs. it meant 0112 hrs. and not 0111 hrs or 0113 hrs – we had to be there on the minute and, so, again, accurate navigation was vital. Changing weather conditions could cause a 'plane to fly ahead or behind time but, as the range of airspeeds was limited, the navigator had to anticipate, well in advance, any possible alterations to E.T.A. and make any necessary adjustments to course and speed to arrive on time.

Thirdly, it was argued that the bomber stream must keep to a pre-arranged track, or route, at a prescribed height. Safety from fighter attack lay in numbers. A stray bomber, away from the main stream, was easy prey for the night fighters but in the stream itself there were hundreds of air gunners looking out for night fighters. Again, it was vital for the navigator to keep on track. The route to the target was never direct. Individual squadrons and whole bomber groups would rendezvous at a turning point such as Skegness or Mablethorpe for No.1 Group and then alter course for the next leg, perhaps over the sea, where they would meet up with the rest of main force. Sometimes Pathfinder Force would mark the turning points with coloured flares. The route would try to avoid crossing over areas or cities heavily defended by flak and also tried to steer clear of night fighter bases. Yet, again, accurate navigation was essential – being just a few miles off track could lead a 'plane into murderous flak.

The same routine applied on the return flight – bombers could just as well be shot down empty as with full bomb loads. Hence, the navigator was working flat out from take off to landing as, of course, was the rest of the crew – each with his own particular job. With Gee and H2S the navigator was constantly fixing his position, calculating new wind velocities and ground speeds, alterations of course and E.T.A.s. He would warn pilot and crew of hazards en route such as approaches to the enemy coast, heavily defended areas and high ground and inform them of turning points and E.T.A.s. On my particular squadron, a small camera was attached to the H2S receiver which was used to take pictures of the P.P.I. at precise intervals on the run up to the target until the bomb aimer called: "Bombs gone!" Hence, the navigator saw very little of the actual bombing of the target.

From Lindholme we were posted to No. 1 Lancaster Finishing School at Hemswell for a short course to familiarise ourselves with the Lancaster. In my case I much preferred the navigator's position in the main cabin behind the pilot whereas in the Halifax I was down in the nose. From the safety point of view the canopy over the cockpit gave much better all round vision for the pilot and engineer – vital when flying in crowded skies. The navigator's position was screened off by a curtain to prevent light from the angle poise lamp showing outside. Even in daytime the curtain was often closed so that it would be easier to read the Gee and H2S screens. The navigator sat at a table facing the port wing which could be seen through a small window. Over the chart table was the astrograph which facilitated the plotting of astro shots. To the left was the "Gee Box" and, to the right, was the H2S. In front, mounted on the fuselage was a duplicate instrument panel housing a compass repeater, air speed indicator, altimeter and the control switches for the D.R. (Distant Reading) compass. Above that was the air position indicator. This was a device which gave the aircraft's position in latitude and longitude assuming there was no wind. Having calculated winds from fixes the navigator would periodically reset the A.P.I. to a new ground position.

The flying programme at Hemswell was short consisting, mainly, of circuits and "bumps." There was one exercise, however, for the gunners called fighter affiliation which gave pilot and gunners practice in "corkscrewing" – evasive action taken to avoid an attacking fighter. If a gunner saw a fighter coming in from, say, starboard he would yell: "Fighter Fighter! Corkscrew starboard Go! "The pilot would immediately throw the Lanc into a twisting dive to the right (starboard) causing the fighter to overshoot. At the bottom of the dive the pilot would open the throttles and climb up to the left (port) so, in theory, the fighter, correcting his overshoot, would overshoot again to starboard. On this occasion, Robbie's corkscrews were so vicious that a gunnery instructor, who was with us, blacked out. When he recovered he said that this had never happened to him before even though he had done a tour of ops. The "attacking" fighter pilot reported that it was impossible to get a burst in at us and this was confirmed when photographs from the "camera gun" were analysed.

Poker recounts Mo's expertise as a bomb aimer. On training flights from Lindholme and, later, on the Squadron there would be practice bombing exercises on a target set up on the sea shore at Wainfleet. The triangular target, with sides fifteen feet in length was painted a bright yellow with a 'hollow' centre with six feet sides. "From 3,000 feet he consistently hit the target with 25% of the practice bombs inside the centre triangle. He was a perfectionist. I remember, on one very rare occasion, when his first bomb missed the target by about five yards, Mo was most aggrieved and accused Art of giving him a duff wind to feed into his bombsight. Art promptly recalculated and came up with the same wind and, on the next bombing run, Mo hit the bull's eye. Over the intercom came fragments of Mo's conversation to himself: 'Maintenance – bloody practice bombs – some people don't care!' Such incidents as these instilled confidence in all of us so that we now really did operate as a united crew – a complete whole."

Poker recalls one other incident during our stay at Hemswell. It seems that he and I had cycled down, the two of us on one bike, to a local snack bar one morning for a mug of tea and a spam sandwich. Returning to camp we were stopped by the local 'bobby'. "In all seriousness this pompous policeman proceeded to lecture us on the dangers of riding two on a bike and then, promptly, booked us. After he had gone we looked at each other in sheer disbelief and Art said, 'If that **** thinks it's dangerous to ride two on a bike he wants to try riding seven in a bloody Lancaster!' With that we both remounted and rode back to camp." The sequel came a few weeks later at Waltham when we learned that we had been fined £5, in our absence, by the magistrates at Lindsey Court."

A couple of days later we were all assembled in the crew room to hear which squadrons we had been posted to. To some extent crews were allowed a choice and Poker, who had served on detachment to 100 Squadron at Seletar, Singapore, suggested to Robbie that we should try for that. The Squadron, which had a very high reputation, did require crews and we felt very happy to be posted to Waltham or, officially, R.A.F. Grimsby. In the middle of September, 1944, we reported to Squadron Leader Irving, the "A" Flight Commander. It had taken over two and a half years to begin my tour of ops!

Chapter Six

100 SQUADRON

Where are the Poles with their gaiety and sadness,
All with the most unpronounceable names.
Silently, ruthlessly, flying in vengeance
Remembering their homes and their country in flames?

R.A.F. Grimsby, or Waltham as it was more generally known, lay between the villages of Waltham and Holton le Clay. Today it is almost unrecognisable as the countryside, as we knew it, has been , largely, built up. Adjoining Waltham today is New Waltham. The Nissen huts housing station personnel have disappeared; most of the station buildings have gone although a few, sorry shells remain. Forty five years ago it was a thriving community. It has been said, that to keep one man in the air, required the services of seven men on the ground Which would give Waltham a population of 1500 or so. It was a happy station. A social centre open to all ranks enabled officers, N.C..O.s and men and women of other ranks to mingle together over a cup of tea, a sandwich or a bun.

Each aircrew trade had its own section such as navigation, radio, bombing and the rest. A fleet of 'bowsers' carried over 50,000 gallons of 100 octane aviation fuel to tank up a couple of dozen Lancasters. Armourers loaded hundreds of tons of bombs from the bomb dump which stored a terrifying variety of bombs. More armourers would service the Browning machine guns in the three turrets of each Lanc and arm them with thousands of rounds of ammunition. Engine and airframe fitters would work day and night, in the open, in all weathers to keep the Lancs airworthy; electricians and radar technicians would service Gee, H2S and radio equipment. Supporting all these were the cooks and catering staff providing meals at all hours of the day and night in the three messes and, to keep us all healthy, was the efficient team of medical staff.

To keep it all running smoothly were the Administrative and Orderly Room Staff; security was the province of the R.A.F. Police and R.A.F. Regiment; there was the M.T. section which provided all manner of transport from 'artics' which moved airframes, to lorries, vans, pickups, cars and the crew bus which took crews out to their 'kites' for ops and back to the crew room and debriefing on their return. There were the girls in the Parachute section with whom we always cracked the same old joke:

"What do I do if it doesn't open?" "Bring it back and I'll give you another one!"

There was the Fire section and the ambulance – always on "Stand by"; the Signals section, Instruments and a host of others – all vital to keeping the Squadron airborne and efficient and the crews happy. And then there was the Intelligence section, who briefed us before an op and debriefed us on our return, and the Meteorology section who did their best to give us the right winds!

In overall charge of the whole station was 'Groupie' – in our time, Group Captain Newbiggin. In command of the Squadron itself was Wing Commander Pattison who was soon succeeded by Wing Commander Hamilton. Squadron Leader Bill Irving was the "A" Flight Commander whilst Squadron Leader Scott was O|C "B" Flight. Navigators were in the charge of Flight Lieutenant Trafford, bomb aimers – Flight Lieutenant

Zaggerman, Wireless Operators – Flight Lieutenant Thompson, Gunners – Flight Lieutenant Donovan Iland whilst Vin Knight had followed us to begin his second tour of ops and take charge of the Flight Engineers. I mention all these because they are the characters named in the Squadron song!

The procedure for operations went something like this. First of all the station was cut off from the outside world for security reasons – no-one could leave or make outside 'phone calls. Armourers and tanker men would report to their sections to organise bomb loads and fuel. The petrol load always gave rise to speculation about the target. Full tanks, 2154 gallons indicated a long trip deep inside Germany whilst 1,400 or so looked like the Ruhr, or 'Happy Valley'. All crews reported to their flight offices to see if they were on the battle order and there would be a short air test of the 'plane when each crew member would check his equipment for serviceability.

About four hours before take off the navigators would be called to their "ops meal" which was usually bacon and eggs – a treat in wartime, rationed Britain. Following the meal they would go to the navigation section with their canvas bags containing plotting instruments for their briefing where, for the first time, they would learn of the target. At the front of the room would be a large wall map with the target and routes, out and back, marked with a ribbon. The Navigation Officer would already have prepared a blackboard showing the position of turning points and the target itself whilst another board would indicate the forecast winds at varying heights along the route. Using the 'Met winds' and the known operational speeds of the Lancaster each navigator would draw up his own flight plan for the operation and, possibly, double check his own figures with a colleague. Additional, relevant information such as radio beacons, hazards and so on would be plotted on the chart and particular points and instructions noted in the log.

About three quarters of an hour later crews would meet up

together for the main briefing in the Ops Room. The Station Intelligence Officer would describe the target and the purpose of the operation; the size of the bomber force; special instructions from Group H.Q. which always seemed to be "Maximum Effort"; he would point out enemy defences and warn of the importance of keeping on time and track. Actual time on target was specified and the Pathfinders' marking technique described. The Met Officer would then give his forecast of weather conditions en route: fronts, icing levels, cloud cover and possible hazards arising from Met conditions on our return. The other section heads would give any other specialised information such as call signs and the letter of the day although the engineers, gunners, bomb aimers and wireless operators would have had their own individual briefings earlier. Individual queries would be answered and, finally, there would be a short 'pep' talk by the Station Commander which always ended with:

"Good luck! Good bombing – and no early returns!"

This last admonition was always sobering. An early return meant that the target had not been attacked by a particular crew which, at the least, would detract from the Squadron's overall bombing statistics and performance. Of course, there could be dozens of reasons for aborting an operation: engine failure, radio and radar faults, crew sickness or a variety of mechanical problems. Despite air tests things still went wrong sometimes – many inexplicable malfunctions were attributed to the "gremlins". Any early return was investigated most thoroughly starting with the relevant section head through to the Flight Commander, Squadron Commander right up to the Station Commander. The skipper would be interrogated and, in some cases, an investigation would be carried right up to Group H.Q. because an "early return" might reflect, not only on the squadron, but on the Group itself. Hence, an aborted operation was not taken lightly.

From briefing the crews went on to collect their flying kit,

'Mae West', parachute harness, parachutes, flying rations, special equipment such as the nav's gear and sextant and their escape kits. The escape equipment consisted of a canvas pouch which contained a map in the shape of a handkerchief, a compass in the form of a stud or a bachelor button, emergency rations and a sum of German or occupied European currency. We also carried a selection of passport type photographs printed in various shades of sepia. The purpose behind these was, should we be trying to escape after baling out or being taken prisoner,to try to contact the underground resistance movement or some escape organisation who would use the photographs to make up false papers. Flying rations consisted of flasks of coffee, chocolate, boiled sweets, sandwiches and chewing gum. Most of us saved the sweets to take home on leave. Poker and Ronnie took charge of the coffee and once we were well clear of the target they would pass it round. Poker developed his own little ritual for Robbie and himself. When about a hundred miles or so from the target on the homeward flight he would pass a cup to Robbie. Forty years on Robbie still insists that Poker's coffee was the best he ever drank.

Once they had collected their gear the crews would make their way to the crew bus. "Crews for J Jig, L Love, A Able!" a W.A.A.F. driver would call out. We would pile into the transport and the driver would take us out to our 'plane parked at a dispersal point. As each crew left the bus there would be calls of: "See you at 4.30!" or, "How about a night on the town tomorrow?" "Keep your finger out!" and the like. Arriving at dispersal Robbie and Poker would check round the aircraft doing the external inspection and chat with the ground crew about any alterations, adjustments, repairs that may have been done. Then, if we had a few minutes to spare, we would probably have a smoke and, maybe, a pee in the hedge before climbing aboard. Once inside we would stow away our parachutes and other gear and make our own pre flight checks. Once settled on my green, leatherette covered bench I would unfold and position my chart on the nav table and set out a selection of well sharpened 3H pencils, Douglas protractor, dividers, ruler, rubber and my Dalton Navigational Computer. Next, we would all plug into the intercom socket and oxygen point and await Robbie and Poker starting up the engines. To conserve batteries a 'trolley accumulator' would be plugged into the electrical system by the ground crew to start up the engines. As Robbie signalled to the ground crew the motors were started in turn. Individual motors provided power for the generators for radio and radar sets and hydraulic power for gun turrets, flaps, bomb doors, elevators, rudder and brakes. When all motors were running smoothly each member of the crew would check his own specialist equipment. I would switch on the master switch of the D.R. compass and adjust the variation to show "True" courses and, one by one, we would report to the Skipper:

"Navigator to Skipper, Gee and H2S O.K. D.R. compass set to True."

The altimeters were set to read zero feet and I would set Waltham's latitude and longitude on the air position indicator. Robbie and Poker would have gone through their own cockpit drill whilst the rest of us were checking our own gear. When all was ready and all had reported "O.K." Robbie would signal to the ground crew, "Chocks away!" and we would slowly taxi out on to the perimeter track to join the queue of Lancs heading for the runway.

At the end of the runway was the ground controller's caravan. When the runway was clear for take off the controller would flash a green Aldis lamp indicating the aircraft letter for take off. As Robbie and Poker advanced the four throttle levers, with the brakes still on, the four Merlins would build up to a roar and the aircraft would vibrate and strain like a dog at a leash to get off down the runway. With the release of the brakes she would quickly gather momentum as the C.O. and an assortment of station personnel gathered to wave:"Goodbye and Good Luck!" from the edge of the runway. Poker would call out the airspeed in knots:

"70 . . . 80 . . . 90 . . . " as Robbie held the Lanc straight and level. At about 110 knots, with throttles 'through the gate' and maximum power thirty six tons of Lancaster would be airborne.

"Undercarriage up!" from Robbie.

"Undercarriage up!" confirmed Poker.

"Climbing power."

Poker would reduce the revs and boost as the Lanc, with undercarriage up, climbed away from Grimsby. As we cleared the runway I would make my first log entry:

"16.36 hrs. Airborne."

Though never a particularly religious person, nevertheless there were three occasions on every op when I said a quick prayer. The first of these was on take off. Behind the navigator on the starboard bulkhead was the flight engineer's instrument panel. On it were four fuel gauges and, amongst a variety of dials, were four fuel pressure warning lights and, below them, four fuel tank selector cocks. The navigator's job on take off was to watch these warning lights like a hawk and, if one came on, to immediately turn the appropriate fuel cock to get fuel through to the engines. Should an engine cut out on take off it could be fatal. The sudden drop in power would cause the Lanc to slew off the runway and crash in a conflagration of 2,000 gallons of petrol and tons of bombs. That minute or so, then, speeding down the runway was critical. This actually happened to a Lanc at Waltham. The crew made a miraculous escape before the Lanc exploded and the navigator is alleged to have remarked, later, "Blast it! There go my new 3H pencils!"

The second occasion was on the run up to the target. Throughout the flight to the target I was kept busy plotting fixes every six minutes with Gee or H2S and amending courses, air speds and the rest. En route I would hear a running commentary over the intercom from the rest of the crew:

"There's a Lanc crossing over from port Skipper!"

"Flak on the starboard bow!"

"There's the flares for the turning point!"

"Jeez! Look at that!" as a bomber, hit by flak, exploded in the sky. Occasionally I would pop my head into the astrodome or stand behind Poker and Robbie to have a look round. Once we were in sight of the target, however, Mo would take over and give Robbie instructions for the bombing run. Sometimes I had a moment to have quick look at the target but then it was back to my bench to take photographs of the PPI on the bombing run. Once on the bombing run 'plane and crew were committed. Apart from the threats from fighters and flak there was the added danger of collision as dozens of bombers were making their own bombing runs over the target. As the 'plane rocked to the "crump" of nearby flak bursts or the slip stream of other 'heavies' close by I felt that this was the moment of truth. As we say in Yorkshire: "It was muck or nettles!"

Mo would go through his drill of:

"Bomb doors open!" With the greater air resistance it felt as though Robbie had put on the brakes – there was a feeling of nakedness with the bomb doors open to the flak below and our own six or seven tons of bombs waiting to be hit. Then, in a cool, calm drawl Mo would go on:

"Right!" or "Left Left!" "Steady . . . Steady. Bombs Gone!"

Robbie would order "Bomb doors closed!" and that was the time I said my second little prayer. Immediately after "Bomb doors closed!" I gave Robbie a course out of the target area when we would dive away at full throttle – it was only then that I felt that we were back in command of the situation. The third occasion was a quick "Thank you!" after we had landed and taxied back to dispersal.

As we approached the circuit on our return and the welcome "GY" lights appeared on the ground Robbie would call up control and ask for permission to land. If a few of us returned together we would be stacked over the airfield until we were given the all clear to land.

"J Jig Downwind!" called Robbie on the R.T.

"J Jig Down wind ." acknowledged control.

"J Jig Funnel!" and down we would go.

At dispersal we would be greeted by the ground crew, Bless 'em! who always waited up for us, to whom we reported any snags or damage and then, very quickly, the W.A.A.F. driver would appear to collect us and take us back for debriefing. Waiting for us would be the C.O., Padre, W.A.A.F.s with hot tea and rum, the section leaders and Intelligence officers. The crew would sit together for debriefing when we would describe the attack, flak, fighters, target indicators, aircraft shot down and anything else relevant to the raid. Our accuracy was assessed the following day by examination of the photographs taken automatically when Mo released his bombs and double checked from my P.P.I. photographs. We would be questioned by our individual section leaders:

"What range did you get from Gee? Any astro shots?"

Navigators would report on weather, winds, cloud and the accuracy of the Met forecasts. The rest of the crew would report to their own sections and we would then return our gear to the locker room and 'chutes to the 'chute section. Intelligence collected our escape kits and then it was off to bacon and eggs and bed!

Chapter Seven

OPERATIONS

"Where are the Kiwis who left all the sunshine
For bleak windy airfields and Fenland and dyke;
Playing wild mess games like 'High Cockalorum'
And knocking the hell out of Hitler's Third Reich?"

Before a crew did its first op it was the practice for the skipper
to fly as 'second dickie' with an experienced crew to get some
experience of the real thing and to learn from the other crew's
expertise. On the 23rd September Robbie went to Neuss. Other
raids that night, involving over 900 aircraft, went to Munster
and the Dortmund Ems Canal. Twenty two aircraft were lost.
The next morning the six of us met Robbie in the Flight Office.
   "What was it like Skip?"
   Robbie looked thoughtful and paused for a moment or two:
"Well, fellers," he replied, "I guess we've still got a lot to learn."
He went on to describe the fires and smoke of the target area,
the probing searchlights and the dull red flashes of exploding
flak. The main lessons were, again, accurate navigation and the
absolute necessity for everyone to keep their eyes peeled from
take off to landing. Each crew member had his own particular
area of vision such as the bomb aimer looking forward and
below; the mid upper gunner, above and around and the rear
gunner above and below with both of them continuously turning

95

their turrets to scan the skies, not only for fighters but to look out for hundreds of other Lancs and Halifaxes in the bomber stream. Whilst the skipper, quite literally, had his hands full the flight engineer would search the skies ahead and above and, through his perspex 'blip', he could also see directly below the 'plane. In the approach to the target area and, when not 'listening out' at his radio, the wireless operator would take up his lookout position in the astro dome.

One other instruction we had received during training was also emphasised – the importance of refraining from idle chatter on the intercom. It was a strict rule that we should only use the intercom when there was a definite message to impart to the skipper or when he wanted to address a particular member of the crew. Unnecessary talk could prevent a vital instruction or warning, such as a fighter attack, being heard. Robbie was a stickler for this and if one of us had, inadvertently, left his microphone switched on the whole crew would hear the sound of heavy breathing followed immediately by: "Mike!" from Robbie. Instantly, six hands would go to check that the mike was switched off. We learned more about the importance of 'window', thousand of strips of metal foil which the bomb aimer threw out by the bundle to fox the enemy radar; more corkscrews had to be practised and Robbie learned to 'weave' and 'jink' on course to make his Lanc an even more difficult target for both enemy flak and fighters.

For much of what follows I am indebted to Poker who, sitting up front with Robbie with his all round vision, saw as much of the action as anyone. On the 26th September we were briefed for our first op in "J – Jig". This, incidentally, was not our own "Jug and Bottle" but an older one on the Squadron. The target was Cap Gris Nez. At this stage of the war our armies had broken out from Caen and were pushing the Germans eastwards out of France. One prong of this was aimed at clearing the Channel ports. We were called at 0600hrs for our pre ops meal of bacon and eggs which was followed by briefing. The target was a German strong point which lay between two converging railway lines. Over 500 heavy bombers were briefed to attack similar targets in the area of the Pas de Calais in a daylight operation under clear, blue September skies.

After collecting our flying kit, 'chutes and escape kits we were driven out to 'J-Jig' where we all went through our pre flight checks as described above. Then, with chocks away, we taxied round the perimeter track to join the queue of Lancs awaiting take off. The main Grimsby Louth road crossed part of the perimeter track and, on this particular day, traffic was halted at the junction on take off. There was a double decker bus waiting at the barrier with its passengers leaning out of the windows waving and cheering us on our way. We all waved back and then it was our turn to take up our position at the end of the runway. At 1030 hrs. we were airborne on our first op climbing to 16,000 feet on course for the French coast. The ninety minute flight was uneventful until the target was in sight when, for the first time, we saw a few bursts of desultory flak until the leading Lancasters started dropping their fifteen, 1,000lb high explosives. Mo found the target easily and, according to the photographs, hit it accurately. In fact, the whole raid was considered successful and the bombing described as accurate and concentrated. Two Lancasters were lost. The following day was almost a carbon copy except that the target was more German fortifications at Calais. We were called at 05.00hrs. and took off at 08.40 with 340 other Lancs. This time the target was obscured by cloud but the Master Bomber ordered the main force down below cloud to bomb the target visually. Again, the bombing results were very good -just one Lancaster was lost.

This was a piece of cake! Two ops and we had hardly been over enemy territory for more than five minutes! As the Squadron song tells:

"We love to nip off smartly to a little buzz bomb site

"And smartly nip off home again and get to bed at night!"

We were soon to face reality. The rest of the month was occupied with more training: fighter affiliation where the gunners tried to "shoot down" an attacking Spitfire or Hurricane whilst Robbie tried to tear the wings off "D – Dog" and "B-Baker" in vicious corkscrews. There were bombing exercises at Donna Nook for Mo and an H2S cross country for me. Similar training occupied the first three days of October with the emphasis on H2S cross countries for me and more bombing for Mo. On the last exercise we returned after an hour because of a faulty compass.

On the 5th October we found ourselves on the battle order for our third op and, shortly after lunch, we were called to briefing. The target was Saarbrucken on the Siegfried Line and the aim of the raid was to assist the American advance by destroying the railway system and supply routes to the town. The bomb load consisted of a 4,000lb. 'cookie' and 8,000lbs. of incendiaries. In effect, the cookie would blast open buidings and the incendiaries would set fire to them. This was our first night operation and, from the outset, Robbie exhorted us all to keep a sharp lookout for other Lancs as nightfall approached. For this trip we were flying in "H – How", or "Hellzapoppin" as its regular crew had christened it. As we were having a last smoke before climbing aboard one of the ground crew tapped Poker on the shoulder and said: "Take good care of her Sarge, she doesn't really care for Canadian Flight Looeys!"

We took off at 18.00 hrs.and climbed to rendezvous with the rest of No. 1 Group Lancasters over Skegness and then headed south east to meet up with the rest of the main force of 530 Lancs. As the sky darkened Robbie warned us to keep a sharp lookout for other Lancs. Plotting my Gee fixes every six minutes gave me reliable winds which necessitated very minor alterations of course. I warned of approaching turning points and gave Robbie a new course to fly when, at the appointed time, the whole stream of bombers would wheel on to the next leg of the flight and, again, Robbie reminded everyone of the need for a careful lookout as hundreds of Lancs altered course. As we approached the enemy coast Mo bundled out window and the crew intensified its search of the night sky – this time for fighter penetration of the bomber force. The outward flight to the target, if one can disregard the tension, was uneventful. At the final turning point, before the run up to Saarbrucken, I gave Robbie the new course and E.T.A. We were flying at 20,000 feet and would soon descend to our bombing height of 16,000. Robbie, Poker and Mo were straining their eyes ahead to get their first glimpse of the target when Mo would take over and direct Robbie to line up "Hellzapoppin" for the bombing run.

"There it is!" bawled out Mo as the target indicators went down in the distance. I quickly popped outside my curtained off position and stood behind Robbie and Poker and stared ahead through the perspex. After three hours, working under the angle poise lamp, my night vision had not had time to adjust to the night sky. Ahead, I could discern a dull red glow thousands of feet below and, above it, what appeared to be pin pricks of red and yellow flashes.

"Left left Skipper." called Mo.

I returned to my position to prepare the P.P.I. camera for shots of the bombing run. Now, over the row from "Hellzapoppin's" four Merlins I could hear a repeated "Crump! Crump!" The Lanc was rocking and bumping like a car on a bumpy road and I heard strange rattles on the fuselage like the sound of gravel thrown at a window. Poker takes up the tale:"The flak was now really awesome – thousands of sparkling shell bursts concentrated in an area above the target indicators between 15,000 and 20,000 feet and there didn't seem to be enough space between the bursting shells for a flying bomb to squeeze through let alone a Lancaster! I couldn't believe we could fly through that and come out at the other side in one piece." We were in the middle of a box barrage, roughly a mile square with searchlights probing the sky by the dozen to seek out the attacking Lancs.

"Do we have to go through that Skipper?" asked Poker.

"Sure," replied Robbie calmly, "We'll press on and it will open out a bit. Keep your eyes open for fighters you guys!"

"Hold it Skipper." called Mo, now cool and calculating as we started on the bombing run. On we flew, straight and level and the 'crumps' intensified in hundreds of distant and not so distant explosions and yellow flashes. The smell of cordite pervaded the cabin. Poker described the scene as a carpet of fires, smoke and flak bursts. The Lanc bounced and lurched to the explosions and the slipstreams of dozens of other Lancs. The 'plane was peppered with shrapnel and one piece clanged through the fuselage, just behind Poker's seat,and embedded itself in my bench seat before doing any further damage!

"Bomb doors open!" called Mo.

"Bomb doors open!" acknowledged Robbie.

The 'plane shuddered with the increased air resistance and I had that feeling of nakedness as the Lanc's bomb bay, over which Ronnie and I sat, lay open and exposed to the bursting flak below. I took my first P.P.I. picture.

"Left . . . left!" called Mo, "Steady . . . Stee..daay . . . Bombs gone!"

"Bomb doors closed!" ordered Robbie.

"Bomb doors closed!" acknowledged Poker.

Robbie threw the Lanc into a diving turn to port on to a new course out of the target area.

"Everyone O.K.?" he called. We all acknowledged in turn.

I gave a new course to rejoin the main force for the flight home and we gradually settled back into our normal routine. As we approached the coast Ronnie and Poker dished out the coffee and the crew began to chat excitedly about the raid. There was many a Canadian expletive:

"Holy shit did you see that flak!"

"I reckon those goddam Krauts got theirs' tonight," observed Mo, dryly. "We were bombing through ten tenths flak!" exclaimed Poker.

"O.K. Cool it fellers!" ordered Robbie, "Keep quiet on the intercom – we're not home yet!"

Nor were we to get home until the next day. On the last leg home, over France, Ronnie came on to the intercom:

"Message from base Skipper. We've been diverted to Stradishall."

Robbie acknowledged and I worked out a new course. In our absence the weather had deteriorated and we wouldn't have been able to land at Waltham. We landed safely at Stradishall where we were given a bacon and egg meal and billets for the night. The next morning we went out to inspect the 'plane and found it peppered with shrapnel holes in the fuselage and tail fins but, as there didn't seem to be any structural damage we took off at 1105 for the half hour flight back to Waltham. On arrival at base we handed the scarred Lanc over to the ground crew to patch up and went off to debriefing.

Recording the account of the Saarbrucken raid in the "Bomber Command War Diaries" the authors, Middlebrook and Everett described it as a big success. The area bounding the railway line was severely damaged, over 600 houses were destroyed and another 1100 badly damaged. The town had been, largely, evacuated but 344 people were killed. Miraculously, only three Lancasters were lost.

The following day, 7th October, we were again on the battle order. The target was Emmerich, a German industrial town, just across the Dutch border and, again, we were flying in "Hellzapoppin." Emmerich and nearby Cleve were towns on the Rhine in the path of the Anglo| Canadian forces near Nijmegen which, according to Middlebrook and Everitt, was threatened by the allied reverses at Arnhem. Hence, the two towns had to be taken out to remove the German threat to the allied front.

After our daylight debut at Calais we felt fairly confident as we prepared to go out to "Hellzapoppin" again. After all, nothing could be as bad as Saarbrucken! We were further relieved to learn that we would have a fighter escort of Mustangs and Thunderbolts. In the event we never even saw them because they had, apparently, ranged well in front of the bomber force to nullify any German fighter opposition. They must have done a good job because we never saw a single one of either friend or foe. Although this was only our fourth op the powers that be must have thought we were no longer a "sprog" crew because we were briefed to go in at 15,000 feet whereas successive waves would bomb from heights up to 20,000 feet.

We took off at 12.10 hrs and, as we so often did, met up with another 340 Lancs over Mablethorpe. There was some light flak over the Dutch coast but, because of the fighter escort, we didn't expect any trouble from the Luftwaffe. Two or three minutes before E.T.A. Mo spotted Emmerich ahead. Our bomb load was the usual cookie and cluster.

"Bomb doors open!"

"Bomb doors open!"

Mo went through his routine guiding Robbie on the bombing run."Cookie gone!" called Mo. (There was a few seconds delay before the incendiaries were released.) Again, Poker takes up the tale:

"There was a fair amount of flak but it wasn't too troublesome and I was searching the sky above and below for possible trouble. On the bombing run I spotted a Lancaster about 500 feet above us drifting in from starboard with its bomb doors open. It was about 100 yards in front of us and we were gaining on it. I shouted to Robbie and pointed at the Lanc above barely fifty yards in front. Just as Robbie looked up its 4,000lb. cookie was released and missed us by about forty yards.

100 SQUADRON. (2 FLIGHTS) — DATE: SATURDAY 7 OCTOBER 1944 — HOONRISE/HOONSET — BLACKOUT FROM 19:?? TO 0749

TRACK MILES	686
PETROL LOAD	1300
BOMB LOAD	1 x 4000 HC, 6 x 150 x 4.lB, 3 x 60 x 4.lB
ALL UP WEIGHT	65115
NAV MEAL	0800
NAV TRANSPORT	0845
NAV BRIEFING	0900
OPERATIONAL MEAL	0845
CREWS TO TECHNICAL SITE	0930
MAIN BRIEFING	0945
CREWS TO AIRCRAFT	1045
TAKE OFF	1200
DEADLINE	1242
FORM G	1401
AIRCRAFT SERVICEABLE	20
CREWS OPERATIONALLY FIT	22
CREWS UNDER TRAINING	5
CREWS ON LEAVE	6
CREWS NON-EFFECTIVE	–
OFFER	8 OCT
DERBY	5/8
GOODWOOD	5/8
GARDENING	–
DETAILED	

CAPTAIN	A/C	TOOK OFF	LANDED	REMARKS RESULT	PHOTO
SECTION I					
F/O Veitch	A²	1200	1551	Primary	T/A
F/O Healy	B	1201	5.55	1620	
F/O George	J	1213	5.51		
F/O Bell	Q	1203	5.57		
F/O Smith		1205	6.04		
F/O Hassler	T	1154	5.53		
W/C Hamilton	U	1158	6.06		
F/O Thomson	W	1204	6.16		
F/O Lenehan	X	1200	6.14		
F/O Hay	Z	1156	6.01		
SECTION II					
F/O Harris	E	1210	1555		
F/O Martin	F	1212	6.08		
F/O Martin	F	1208	6.17		
F/O Griffiths	G	1209	6.00		
F/L Robb	H	1206	6.24		
F/O Stuart	M	1210	5.58		
F/O Ellis	N	1211	6.10		
F/O Falconer	P	1159	6.13		
F/O Edge	R	1207	6.25		
F/O Ladbury		1216	6.03		
F/L Brown	A	1221	6.11		
SECTION III					
F/O McKenzie	D	1220	1559		
P/O Ordell	V	1215	6.07		
P/O Davidson	S	1243	6.12		

Battle order – Emmerich.

'It's O.K.' said Robbie, 'It's well clear.' I was still looking up when the Lanc's incendiaries came down – hundreds of them drifting back towards us. I instinctively ducked down the tunnel leading to the bomb aimer's compartment when I heard a number of dull thuds and a crashing sound. Looking across at Robbie I saw him brushing bits of shattered perspex from his face; there was a great big hole in the windscreen immediately in front of him and an icy wind was blasting straight on to him. I gave him a hand to pull his goggles down to protect his face when there was a shout from Mo:

"We're on bloody fire! Where's all the goddam fire extinguishers?' I handed him the first extinguisher through the flames which were then flaring across the tunnel I had been in a few seconds earlier. He grabbed it, twisted open the valve but, unfortunately, he had it pointing at me and I caught the full force in my eyes temporarily blinding me. However I directed Ronnie to the rest of them which he passed to me and I fed them on to Mo. We were on the last one and the flames looked as bad as ever when, with amazing suddeness, Mo's smoke blackened face appeared in the tunnel. With a grin and a thumbs up he said the fire was out."

Whilst all this had been going on Robbie had ordered "Chutes on!" as a precaution if we had to bail out. He had closed the bomb doors but we still had the incendiaries aboard and we were still heading east into Germany. There wasn't another 'plane in the sky – no Lancasters, no Mustangs, Thunderbolts and, Thank God! no enemy fighters. I hurriedly gave Robbie a course for base direct – there was no point in sticking to the flight plan at this stage – and Robbie gingerly turned Hellzapoppin around on to a north westerly heading. I called out the headings from my repeater compass as Robbie banked round to port as his own compass was wrecked. When we had settled on to the new course the rest of the crew surveyed the damage. We knew we had been hit several times but had no idea of the extent of the damage apart from the instrument panel and Mo's compartment. One incendiary had just missed Monty in the mid upper turret and gone out the side of the 'plane. Just then Monty called out that there was smoke coming from both wings.

"I took a long look at both wings," said Poker, "which had a number of holes punched through the top surfaces and, sure enough, smoke seemed to be coming out. We opened up the engines in a dash to get over friendly territory and the smoke appeared to get worse. It was then I realised the holes were directly over the main tanks and it was petrol vapour that was streaming from the wings. Robbie agreed so we reduced power and returned home at a more sedate pace whilst I kept an eagle eye on the fuel gauges."

Nevertheless we kept our 'chutes on and were on standby to jump if the position got any worse. I occasionally checked Robbie's course from my compass giving any necessary corrections and we began heading back over the North Sea.

"What's our airspeed Art?" asked Robbie.

"165 knots." I replied.

I was busy working out a new course and E.T.A. for Grimsby.

"What's our height Art?"

"Nine thousand feet Skip. Hey! Haven't you got any bloody instruments at all up there?" I grumbled, resenting all these interruptions to my calculations. I felt a tap on my shoulder. It was Poker.

"Here you are, Art," he said, and passed me Robbie's altimeter which had been knocked out of the instrument panel! Suitably chastened, I apologised and regularly gave Robbie heights and airspeeds all the way back to Grimsby. Despite the remains of his windscreen icing up, which he cleared using a file from Poker's tool kit, Robbie now felt it was worth while to have a bash at getting back to base. We still kept our 'chutes on because, if the hydraulics didn't work when we were preparing to land, we would have to jump and let Hellazapoppin crash into the sea. As we approached the Humber estuary Robbie commenced the descent as I called out the height:

"8,000 . . . 7,500 . . . 7,000 . . . 6,000 . . . "

We levelled out at about 3,000 feet and Robbie called up control who were getting worried as we were already about thirty minutes late. He described our problems and decided to attempt a landing if the undercarriage could be lowered.

"Undercarriage down!" called Robbie.

"Undercarriage down!" acknowledged Poker.

"Undercarriage locked!" called Poker."O.K. fellers!" shouted Robbie, "Take up crash positions. Art, call out my heights and airspeed as we make the approach!" He brought the battered Lanc down to 1,000 feet over the circuit.

"Airspeed 130 . . . 120 . . . " I called.

"Down wind!" called Robbie to control over the R.T.

"Down wind!" acknowledged control.

"Funnel!"

"Funnel!"

"Airspeed 115 . . . 110 . . . " I called.

It was all up to Robbie now. I climbed over the main spar and took up my crash position with head forward and hands clasped at the back of my neck. "Hellzapoppin" flopped on to the deck like a huge, exhausted Canadian wild goose. The load of incendiaries made sure that she stayed down without a bounce as we belted down the runway at 90 knots, the tyres screaming in protest. It wasn't over yet as we didn't know whether the brakes would work. Speeding alongside us was the crash wagon, ambulance, fire engine and the C.O.s car. Robbie had cut the power and now, gingerly applied the brakes. They worked! 70 . . . 60 . . . 50 . . . we stopped at the end of the runway and then turned along the perimeter track to dispersal. Bedlam broke out on the intercom.

"Bloody good show Skip!"

"That was the best landing you ever made!" cried out Ronnie.

106

"O.K. guys," said Robbie, " but don't forget we've still got those incendiaries aboard. They're still hanging up in the bomb bay!"

As we switched off at dispersal the ground crew were already clambering over that poor, wounded Lanc. We climbed out and were met by the Squadron Commander who had landed half an hour earlier. Walking round poor old "Hellzapoppin" we surveyed the damage. We knew about the bomb which came through the windscreen and the one that narrowly missed Monty. Another had almost severed the elevator control rod whilst another had, similarly, partly severed the rudder controls which were hanging on by a fraction of an inch. An incendiary bomb was found rolling around in five of the six fuel tanks and, altogether, we had been hit by thirteen of them.

Mo and Robbie stood, describing our exploits to a circle of ground crew, the Wingco and a group of others who had joined us whilst the rest of the crew made a fuss of Robbie and Mo. The least we expected was an immediate award of the D.F.C. to them both! Poker recalled the ground crew member's remark on our previous trip: "Hellzapoppin didn't care for Canadian Flight Looeys!"

"How true it turned out," said Poker, "but at least our Canadian Flight Looey had won the battle."

Finally, as the crew bus drew up to take us to interrogation, we were all somewhat deflated as the Wing Commander addressed Robbie:

"Mmm – Well, Robbie, maybe next time you'll look up!"

We later learned of several similar incidents. One crew came home with a 1,000lb high explosive bomb wedged between its starboard engines and many a bomber failed to return because of hits by our own bombs. Harsh as the Wingco's comment seems, he was probably right. For a while we had to take a lot of ribbing from the other crews being the only crew on the Squadron to come back with more bombs than we set off with! We also learned that Flight Lieutenant Art Green, Robbie's pal, and his crew who had joined Pathfinder Force, were shot down over Emmerich although they all baled out safely.

And so ended Op No. 4. "Hellzapoppin" was dismantled and sent off to the maintenance unit. A few days later Flight Sergeant Brown and his crew returned from leave and were shocked and dismayed at the loss of their kite.

"What have you done with our mascot, the little black golliwog?" asked Stamper who had spent hours painting the name on the 'plane. None of had even seen it. Stamper and the rest of his crew went to search the maintenance unit but it was never found. For a few days there was a bit more mickey taking in the mess and social centre until one flyer piped up:

"Well, what the hell did you expect with a bloody name like that?"

Chapter Eight

GETTING ON WITH IT

"Where are they now, these young men of all nations
Who flew though they knew not what might lie ahead,
And those who returned with their mission accomplished
And next night would "beat up" the 'Saracen's Head'?"

After Emmerich I suppose we could, at least, consider ourselves blooded. The idea that any op could be a 'piece of cake' was completely erased from our minds. From the outset none of us had taken the concept of a tour of ops lightly but, now, there was a new sense of seriousness in all of us; an even more sober approach to the task in hand; there was that little extra care in pre flight checks; we would discuss tactics picked up from other crews and, even on our occasional bike rides to the local pubs, we talked a lot of 'shop'. No longer was it simply a matter of getting there, keeping on track and time, bombing and coming home – we also had to keep our eyes peeled for the rest of the bomber force and not only on the run up to the target. On one occasion we saw two Lancs collide and explode in a holocaust of red and yellow flames and black smoke at the first turning point on the Lincolnshire coast long before they had reached operational height. From now on we all searched the skies around us so far as our duties allowed. From the beginning of the tour Robbie refused to use 'George', the automatic pilot, so that he could react instantly to any emergency that arose. That second or two, switching from 'George' to manual, could be a matter of life or death.

About this time a system of categorising crews as "A", "B" or "C" was introduced. It was based on the general performance of crews but with particular reference to a crew's proficiency in bombing. Account was taken of practice bombing results and the flash photos taken of the aiming point at bomb release over the target area. Thanks to Mo's dedication and uncanny skill we found ourselves in category "A" which meant, in practice, that we would be at the forefront of an operation bombing from the "lower deck", as Poker called it, about 15,000 feet. October was to be a month when, to coin a phrase, "they tried to fly our arses off." Two days after Emmerich we were training again. Another H2S cross country for my benefit, bombing practice for Mo and more fighter affiliation for Robbie, Monty and Gibby. We all felt the effects of 'G' forces in our stomachs as Robbie dived, twisted and weaved Lanc "Able 2" about the skies whilst I would curse as my precious 3H pencils disappeared all over the kite whilst computer, dividers, ruler and protractor slid up and down the cabin floor.

On the 11th October we were called, just before lunch, for a daylight on Fort Frederich Hendrik gun batteries at Breskens on the Scheldt estuary in Holland. On the ground British and Canadian forces were trying to flush out the Germans from the Low Countries and this was a target in their path that had to be taken out. In parentheses I should add that, at this stage of the war, General Eisenhower had first call on Bomber Command for tactical bombing although the strategic offensive still continued. Our bomb load consisted of 15,000lbs of high explosives. The route was straight forward over the North Sea to the batteries on the coast at Breskens. 160 Lancs took part in the raid but we, in the second wave, arrived to find the target covered with smoke and dust and, on the master bomber's instructions, we returned to base with our bomb load. At 03.00 hrs. the following day we were called to have another go at it. We took off at 06.10hrs and by 07.30 we had bombed the target accurately.

Two days later began, what I called, the 'Duisburg Weekend."' On the 14th we were called at 03.00 for a daylight on Duisburg which was a big, inland city and inland port in the Ruhr – rather like Manchester. The Ruhr itself, or 'Happy Valley' as the aircrew called it, was the heart of German industry and one of the most heavily defended areas of Germany. This attack was part of "Operation Hurricane" laid on to prove the overwhelming superiority of Bomber Command and the 8th U.S. Air Force. It was to be a decisive, heavily concentrated attack on the densely populated Ruhr. We took off at 06.45 with 15,000lbs of H.E.s and joined over 1,000 Lancasters and Halifaxes as we rendezvoused and headed out over the North Sea. The sky was literally full of heavy bombers with their escorts of swarms of Mustangs and Thunderbolts which could be seen for miles in the beautiful, clear morning air. Regularly, Ronnie, Gibby, Monty or Poker would warn of a Lanc or Halifax edging crabwise above us. As we approached the target, around 08.30, we saw the first target indicators go down just before the first wave arrived. We also saw the flak which was as awesome and concentrated as it had been at Saarbrucken. Ahead, above and below there would suddenly appear a huge, dull red flash and an enormous pall of oily black smoke. "Able 2" rocked with each explosion as Lancasters and Halifaxes were blasted out of the sky in fragments. Poker, himself, counted fourteen of them. The smell of the explosions, acrid to the nostrils, pervaded the whole aircraft.

Up front, in the second wave, we once more started a bombing run and again, right on time, Mo got his target. That minute or so on the bombing run was always the most tense period of the whole op. From "Bomb doors open" Mo calmly, indeed almost

111

laconically, went through his litany of "Left left" or "Right" or "Steady". Sometimes we would hear a murmur such as "Stay there you beauty" or "Gotcha you bastard" but even so the time seemed interminable and the rest of us would be willing him to drop the bloody things and let's get the hell out of there. Unscathed we dived out of the target area and headed back home and , on the way, passed hundreds of American B.17 Flying Fortresses heading out for the same target. The American Air Force, which was designed for daylight raids, always flew in a tight formation. R.A.F. Bomber Command was, primarily, a night striking force and daylight ops, on a large scale, were a fairly recent innovation. Consequently we had never trained to fly in formation but grouped together, somewhat haphazardly, in what was known as a "gaggle" behind a "V" of three leaders thus resembling a gaggle of geese. One thing was sure, the Yanks would have no trouble finding the target!

At 11.30 we landed at base, had our rum and coffee, interrogation, bacon and eggs and returned to our billets where we immediately dived into bed.. The same evening we were called again and, again, it was to be Duisburg. We collected our gear, coffee and rations and drove out to "Able 2" for the second time that day. At 00.10 on the 15th we took off and again set course for Duisburg although, this time, we took a rather different route. Pathfinders were to mark the target but, in the event, there was little need for them as we could see the fires over 100 miles away. The outward flight was uneventful apart from, as Poker relates, "some clot in the bomber stream who was flying with his navigation lights on." Needless to say we tried to keep well away from him! We approached the target on schedule and on track and saw the T.I.s go down in the middle of the conflagration below. There was no sign of flak or searchlights.

"Fighter! Fighter! Corkscrew port GO!" roared Gibby down the intercom. Robbie almost threw the Lanc out of the sky. Down we went in a screaming dive to port and then, with a sickening twist,the nose came up as he did a climbing turn to starboard, So swift and savage was Robbie's corkscrew that neither Monty nor Gibby got a chance to fire at the Junkers 88.

"Can you see anything Monty... Gibby... Ron... Anyone?" shouted Robbie. After a moment or two:

"No signs of it Skip – but it was an 88."

"O.K. but keep your eyes peeled."

We climbed back up to bombing height and, after a slight alteration of course, Mo took over for the bombing run. The rest of the op was uneventful but there was no longer a city of Duisburg. Poker described the scene as a gigantic mass of glowing coals on the bed of an enormous blast furnace. Crossing the coast Poker handed Robbie his coffee:

"Gee, Poker," said he, "this is better than Champagne." We landed at 05.40 and. after more bacon and eggs, went to bed.

Forty two years later Gibby recalled the attack by the 88.

"It was pitch black and I couldn't see a damned thing. For some, short time I had sensed that there was something there behind us – I could feel its presence. Robbie corkscrewed so viciously I was thrown up and banged my head on the top of the turret and it was sore for weeks. Neither Monty nor I could get a shot at it but it was there – I could almost touch it.

At about three in the afternoon we were called yet again. This time the target was the German naval base at Wilhelmshaven. We took off at 17.40 in "Able 2" and were back at base by 22.00 hrs. after another successful and, this time, uneventful raid. In that weekend we had flown three major ops in forty eight hours. Four days later we took off at 16.43 for Stuttgart. This was a very heavily defended target and was the longest trip we had done so far taking almost seven and a half hours. We flew in "L – Love" or " 'ell for Leather" as it was more affectionately known. According to Poker this 'plane had the best set of engines on the Squadron. For the technically minded it was the only Mark 1 Lanc on the Squadron at the time – the others were Mark IIIs with Packard engines. The Mark 1 had Rolls Royce Merlins and 'paddle blade' props. Poker regarded "'ell for Leather" with affection and often recalls how it gave 18lbs. of boost at 3,000 r.p.m. and belted down the runway, with a full load, like a scalded cat. The target was the Bosch works at Stuttgart. Again we encountered the box barrage of heavy flak and dozens of searchlights but we got through it without mishap and Mo added another 'aiming point' to his collection.

Four nights later, on the 23rd, we were briefed for one of the toughest targets in the Ruhr – Essen. This was the heaviest of the many raids on Essen with 1055 aircraft taking part. Our aiming point was the famous Krupps works and, as a result of this raid and a subsequent one two days later, Essen ceased to be a centre of German war production. Again, the trip was uneventful from the point of view of damage to ourselves. We still experienced the same stress and tension as the Lanc bounced along in the slipstreams and we heard and smelled the exploding flak. I, personally, still experienced that 'tight' feeling when the bomb doors opened which was only relieved when Mo released his load and the Lanc jumped several feet in the air in apparent relief at having lost six or seven tons of its burden. The rest of the crew saw the fires and the flak whilst I, in my screened off compartment, sensed it through the comments on the intercom and the bumping of " 'ell for Leather" as she bounced and swayed to the flak bursts. I had learned to discern changes by other senses than my eyes. Changes in engine note as the revs were adjusted for climbing power or the quieter drone for straight and level flight. Gee and H2S were my eyes. An "X" with a 3H pencil plotted our position on a chart and, with the aid of my navigational computer, I could predict where we would be from minute to minute. I regularly informed the crew of our position giving E.T.A.s for the coast, our's or the enemies, turning points, the target and, the most welcome, base. Gibby, alone and remote from the rest of us in his rear turret, would regularly call up:

"How long before we're home Art?"

October drew to a close with a daylight attack on Walcheren, an island in the Netherlands. Our target was one of the German gun positions which were still thwarting the British and Canadian advance. These allied forces were still trying to clear the Scheldt estuary to open up the port of Antwerp. Strangely, when we were approaching the target, the master bomber called off the operation. The Germans had recently destroyed the dykes and partially flooded the island so maybe the master bomber thought that further bombing would do more harm than good to the allied cause. Later, Mo often said we should have gone in and bombed because those guns were still firing at us until the end of the war. However, we ended October with twelve ops in the log book – getting on for half a tour – and went off for a well earned leave.

The first shock we received on our return from leave was that Robbie now sported another 'ring' on his sleeve. Our Flight Commander, Squadron Leader Irving had finished his tour and Robbie had been promoted to "A" Flight Commander. We all, naturally, showered him with our congratulations and it provided us with an excuse, not that we ever needed one, to go out for a few pints to celebrate! We were well accustomed, by now, to hobnobbing with a Flight Looey but a Squadron Leader was a different matter – it was one step nearer God. Ronnie, in his own inimitable manner and Geordie accent tested the water by saying:

"Hey Skip, how does it feel to be a 'Squabbling Bleeder? Robbie took it all in good part with just a grin and:

"Watch it Brownie!"

The bad news was that our rate of ops was to be sharply reduced. At the time we went on leave some of us speculated on getting the tour finished by Christmas or early in the New Year. As Flight Commander, Robbie was expected to serve some appreciable time in his position in order to give some stability to the Flight and there were also occasions when Flight Commanders had to stand in for the Squadron Commander. In practice it meant that our ops would be reduced to two or three per month which wasn't a pleasant prospect. There was always that feeling of having a certain number to do and the satisfaction of crossing another off the list until we had No. 30 in the log book when we would be grounded for a few months. It was rather galling to see new crews coming along and gradually overtaking our score and getting their own tours finished. In the event it didn't work out quite as bad as we expected. Winter was approaching and flying was much curtailed bringing its frustrations to everyone.

Chapter Nine

WINTER 1944–1945

"The Lancs are no more, they are part of the legend,
But memory stays bright in the hearts of the men
Who loved them and flew them through flak and hellfire
And managed to land them in England again."

There is no colder place in Britain than a Lincolnshire airfield in winter. Interspersed with the occasional clear, sharp mornings when we would pedal our bikes down to the Flight Office to see what was happening were days and days of mist, fog, snow, frost and drizzle. As the wags would say:

"The fog's so thick that even the birds can't get airborne!"

These were the days of frustration for all the crews. Ops were called and then cancelled. On some days we even got to the point of starting up the engines, keyed up for an op deep inside Germany, when the cancellation came through over the R.T. It was a period of tension when it seemed that, even, nature was playing a cat and mouse game with us. Eighteen ops to do. We would be keyed up at briefing and then came the anticlimax – ops were scrubbed. On the one hand, the pressure was off for another twenty four hours so we could have a night out, visit a cinema, relax in the social centre, write a letter home or simply go to bed. On the other hand there were still eighteen more to do.

117

We would hang around the Flights and Sections keeping up to date with new developments. Ronnie was the one who seemed to get all the latest news, not only from the Squadron, but from all over the group. It was from Ronnie that I first heard of the death of my two old buddies, Bert Thomas and Sid Pick. Sid was the first to go. After we parted at O.T.U. it seems there was some delay in crewing up and, in effect, he re-crewed. That in itself would be unsettling. On his fourth or fifth op, to Dusseldorf, on the 3rd November, 1944, he was shot down. Bert lasted just a little bit longer. His 'plane crashed on take off for a raid on Cologne on Christmas Eve. The fully laden Lanc exploded and the whole crew were killed.

Meanwhile, life at Waltham went on. Wednesday was sports day and, amongst other activities, the sections organised soccer competitions. Poker and Ronnie played for their respective sections and Poker was selected for the Squadron team to play in the Group knock out competition. He recalls how the team was 'conned' out of winning their match against North Killingholme, the home of 550 Squadron. "550 agreed to pick us up in a crew bus from the railway halt at Killingholme at 13.00 hrs. After hanging around for a while in the cold, wet drizzle one of the team 'phoned 550 to see what was happening and was told a bus would pick them up in a few minutes. It so happened there was a little pub nearby with a lovely fire burning in the grate so we trooped in for an odd pint. The bus still didn't come so we had two or three more! At 14.30 it turned up and we just had time to change and get to the loo before the kick off at 15.00. In the first thirty minutes we were winning three nil but then the agony started! By half time we were desperate and the only cover, away from the spectators, who included a number of W.A.A.F.s, was a clump of bushes about fifty yards behind the goal posts. The whole team made a beeline for the bushes whilst those, not too badly afflicted, made a screen for the more unfortunate. Half way through the second half the pangs returned again and the team moved slower and slower – almost to a stop. 550 won by four goals to three. When their team organiser came to the dressing room to comiserate he was assailed by a hail of well aimed football boots and had to dive for cover."

During that winter of '44|'45 there were quite a few official "stand downs". On those occasions when the powers that be knew there wasn't a hope of flying there would be an official announcement of a twenty four or forty eight hour stand down. Such announcements were greeted with joy because the crews, for once, knew where they were and it was an opportunity for them to really let their hair down. Hundreds of tales have been told of the antics that went on these occasions – many of them emanating from the Officers' Mess. On one occasion a newcomer to the Squadron, an Australian, heard that Robbie was the champion beer drinker and challenged him to a competition. The Aussie lined up a few pints on the bar whilst Robbie lined up the equivalent in halves. The Aussie finished his whilst Robbie was on the last half. 'Groupie', who had been watching the contest, came up to Robbie and slapped him on the back saying: "Good show Robbie!" causing Robbie to throw back the last two pints narrowly missing Groupie's tunic.

On another occasion a group of pilots and section heads went for a night out at a dance hall in Cleethorpes. Robbie, wearing a parson's dog collar with his uniform caused quite a stir with the girls but was apparently outdone by 'Ziggy' Zaggerman, the bombing leader. 'Ziggy' had replaced his bomb aimer's "B" brevet with a "Z". The girls were fascinated.

"What's the "Z" for?" asked one. "I've seen the "O", the "E", "N", "A.G." but I've never seen a "Z" "

"Shush dear," replied Ziggy, "Highly secret."

The following morning rumours were going around the Flight Office that the officers had overstepped the mark and that there would be an inquisition by the Air Commodore up at Base H.Q.

Sure enough, at 10.00 the office 'phone rang. For once, Robbie was quaking in his boots.

"Is that you Robb? What's this I hear about your disgraceful exhibition in Cleethorpes last night?" Robbie started to stammer out a reply when he heard a faint chuckle at the other end of the 'phone.

"It's you Scottie – you lousy bastard! Y'know you scared the shit out of me!" Scottie, Squadron Leader Scott, was Robbie's counterpart as "B" Flight Commander doing a good impersonation of the Base Commander.

Another Mess favourite on standowns was to bring a horse into the Mess for a bucket of beer. On one occasion an officer brought in a donkey from the adjoining farm. Early next morning it was found wandering around the airfield and a young lad came to complain to Groupie. The C.O. assembled all his officers and berated them for their lack of thought and then ordered a whip round to make some gesture of compensation. "You know, Art," said Robbie, "I guess we raised enough to buy the kid half a dozen donkeys!"

When not on the battle order we would sometimes get designated as "Window Crew". This involved collecting a three ton lorry at the stores with the loading details for aircraft carrying window – packets of thousands and thousands of metallized strips of foil which were thrown out of the aircraft at various points on the track to fox the enemy radar. The driver would take us to each dispersal where we would load up the Lanc with its allotted amount. On a long trip much of the spare space in the aircraft would be filled from the front turret to the fuselage. In the meantime we would hang around the Flights and Sections, get a 'cuppa' from the N.A.A.F.I. trolley or cycle down to a shack at the end of the runway at the Holton le Clay end and buy a sandwich, a cuppa and a newspaper. Everyone in those days wanted to see the "Daily Mirror" to see if "Jane" had got all her clothes off yet! Another favourite was the "Daily Express" crossword which wasn't too demanding! From the beginning we searched the newspapers for articles on the previous day's raid cutting out sections which reported operations in which we had been involved. Some of us made a scrapbook of our cuttings-I never did find out what happened to mine.

When we first went to Waltham, Robbie did two ops as "second dickie" although it was some time before we realised he had done an extra one. In any case we were all one or two ops behind him on our tours and these were made up by replacing a crew member in another crew as the occasion arose. Ronnie and Gibby, for example, did trips to Zeitz and Leipzig whilst I did one to Bottrop. None of us felt very happy about flying with a strange crew because, as Poker puts it, our own crew felt like "family". We understood each other and knew what Robbie expected of us. Poker recalls his own "spare bod" trip on a daylight to Essen.

Intercom discipline in our crew was rigid. As Robbie pointed out, any unnecessary chatter on the intercom could be fatal as the skipper or, indeed, any crew member could miss a vital piece of information which could be a matter of life or death. Quite inadvertently some of us would forget to switch off our microphones and the sound of heavy breathing would be heard over the intercom. There would be an instant shout of 'MIKE!' from Robbie to silence the offender. Poker goes on to say: "On this trip I found things totally different. From take off to landing my ears were assailed by a cacaphony of sound as the different crew members chattered or argued with each other over the intercom talking about anything but the job in hand. The only mark of credit I could give them went to the bomb aimer. We were bombing on sky markers with a load of 15 X 1000 pounders when I saw a Lanc, which was also on its bombing run, about 500 feet below and drifting across our path. It seemed as if he was in imminent danger of collecting our bombs if he didn't alter course. He didn't. I ducked down the tunnel so that I could see our bomb aimer, switched on my mike and shouted to him to look out for the Lanc underneath. He looked round and gave me a 'thumbs up' and held back the distributor arm until the Lanc had cleared. I wondered, afterwards, if that crew managed to survive a tour of ops as their look out system was abysmal. So much for my 'spare bod' trip. I was relieved to get it over and vowed that I would never fly with that lot again."

On the 9th November we were airborne on ops again at 08.00 for a daylight attack on Wanne Eickel. At this stage of the war the attention of Bomber Command was directed towards the bombing of oil refineries which were to be our target on this occasion. We finally broke cloud at 22,000 feet over the French coast. At briefing we had been ordered to bomb, if necessary, on H2S. When we arrived in the target area we found the Pathfinder sky markers disappearing into the cloud below so Robbie ordered me to make the bombing run on H2S. I was confident I had identified Wanne Eickel, in the middle of the sprawling Ruhr conurbation, on my radar screen and gave Robbie a heading for the target area – it was impossible to identify the refinery. Mo, in his compartment, had selected the bombs, bomb doors were open and the rest was up to me. At the side of my nav table was a press button switch, or 'tit', rather like the old bedroom 'lazy switch'. Holding the switch I watched the ground echoes on the screen enter the range ring and gauged the time to bomb release.

"Let 'em go Art!" bawled Robbie and Mo. "The others are bombing now!" Alongside us other Lancs were releasing their loads and turning for home.

"Hang on!" I called, "we're not quite there."

A few more seconds passed and I could sense the rest of the crew getting keyed up. I considered we were over the target and pressed the tit.

"Bombs gone!" I called.

"Bomb doors closed!" ordered Robbie.

"Bomb doors closed." from Poker.

We turned to port out of the target and I gave Robbie a course for the first leg home. I don't know to this day whether or not I hit Wanne Eickel. Neither do I know whether the rest of the force did. According to Middlebrook and Everitt the master bomber ordered main force to bomb any built up area. After the war Wanne Eickel itself reported that only two buildings were destroyed with four civilians and six foreign workers killed. We landed "K" King at base at 13.02 – at least we had got No.13 out of the way!

The following day we flew for fifteen or twenty minutes on an air test taking the newly repaired "H" How which had been practically rebuilt since our unforgettable trip to Emmerich. In fact, at first, we didn't realise it was the same 'plane as Stamper's 'Hellzappoin' had been painted out following repairs to the fuselage and a new coat of camouflage paint. On the 16th November we found ourselves on the battle order again and in due course we were called to briefing. This time we were supporting the American army in its advance to the Rhine. The target was Duren, midway between Aachen and Cologne, and it was one of three towns standing in the way of the American advance. Briefing was at 09.30 and we learnt that this was to be a precision attack by "A" category crews. The actual target was a cross roads where two major roads met and were being heavily used by German armoured columns. Over 480 Lancs carrying 1,000 lb. H.E.s were to take part, a master bomber would be in charge of the operation and the target would be marked by "Oboe" Mosquitos.

Robbie had at last managed to get a new Lanc which we could call our own, "J" Jig, which we christened, appropriately enough, "Jug and Bottle" and this was to be her first trip. As we approached the target in brilliant sunshine we saw the markers go down straddling the centre of the crossroads below. We, in the first wave, were called in by the master bomber to bomb the

'Jug and Bottle'

centre of the T.I.s. Although flak was fairly heavy Poker remarked that he had seen a lot worse and Mo took us in on the bombing run. Ahead, there was an excellent concentration of bombs on the crossroads and then it was Mo's turn.

"Bombs gone!" called Mo as "Jug and Bottle" leaped upwards, seven tons lighter. "Bullseye! That'll show the Yanks and their bloody Norden bomb sight!"

Poker recalls this raid with something approaching glee. Complimenting main force on its accuracy the master bomber called out, on the R.T.

"Oh beautiful bombing chaps! Beautiful bombing – but can we now spread them around a little!" Poker, with a delighted grin, commented: "The bombs were all going down the same hole!"

It was later revealed that Duren was virtually wiped out with a large number of casualties. We lost three Lancs. We also learned that the American tanks had been bogged down by mud delaying their advance. The success of this operation confirmed Bomber Command's views that, given fighter escorts, the R.A.F. was every bit as capable of daylight precision bombing as the Americans.

The Duren raid appeared to have completed our quota for November for, although the Squadron did five or six more ops, we didn't find ourselves on the battle order. The only other flying we did was on the 29th when Robbie, always eager to oblige, offered his crew to the Station Commander who wanted to keep his hand in with a spot of local flying. And so, at four in the afternoon, the crew bus dropped us off at dispersal alongside "F" Fox where we awaited the arrival of 'Groupie'. A few minutes later he arrived in a Hillman pickup driven by a W.A.A.F from the M|T section. Almost before she was out of sight he began to pee against the starboard tyre and, in full flow, he turned to us:

"Hello gentlemen, you'll have to excuse me but I always do this before take off. It brings good luck. Squadron Leader Robb's boys I presume?" Groupie was a rather short man but he had a humorous glint in his eye and was a good sport. "I've had good reports about you from Squadron Leader Robb but no doubt he is biased! Now then, let's get this old lady upstairs and see how she performs."

Unknown to me at the time the experience put years on Poker. After the usual pre flight checks we went hurtling down the runway and, being only lightly laden, were airborne with the undercarriage up before reaching the control tower. Groupie climbed to about 8,000 feet and then did a few banking turns, a couple of stalls and a corkscrew or two and then levelled out again at 8,000. Over the intercom came:"Pilot to engineer – feather the starboard outer." Poker promptly complied and, almost immediately, came the order to feather the port outer. We flew along for a minute or two then:"Feather the port inner." Again Poker complied and stepped up the power on the remaining, starboard inner engine. Poker was getting a bit worried that Groupie might want to feather the remaining engine and put the Lanc into a glide but then came the order to unfeather the three Merlins which Poker did with a sigh of relief. When all were running and synchronised Poker gave Groupie the thumbs up and Groupie gave him a deliberate wink as if to say, "I know what you were thinking young man!" We flew back to base and landed to find Groupie's W.A.A.F. driver waiting for him at dispersal. He gave us a cheery wave and, "Well done chaps." and was whisked away in the pickup.

On the 3rd December we found ourselves on the battle order for a precision daylight operation which would take us half way through our tour. Around 03.30 hrs. we were called for briefing for an attack on the Urft dam which was a large reservoir in the Eifel. The destruction of the dam was needed, apparently, to prevent the Germans releasing its waters to flood areas in the path of the American advance. There was considerable excitement at the prospect of this raid following, as it seemed, in the wake of Guy Gibson's "Dam Busters." We were airborne at 07.56 in "Jug and Bottle" on a crisp, clear December morning but, as we progressed south east, cloud gradually built up and we arrived to find the target completely obscured so the master bomber ordered us home again.

The following day we were again on the battle order – this time for Karlsruhe, an important industrial city north west of Stuttgart. German industry had been dispersed deeper and deeper inside Germany which meant a flight of six and a half hours. Our route took us south east through France turning due east, just south of Metz, and avoiding Saarbrucken where we had received our 'baptism of fire' three months earlier. We took off in "Jug and Bottle" at 16.35 hrs and were on the bombing run just before 20.00hrs. The only incident of note was when, well on the way to the target, we saw some clot in the bomber stream flying along with his navigation lights on! Because of strict R.T. silence there was no way of warning him so we gave him a wide berth until he drifted out of sight. Although we didn't see any fighters the flak was, again, heavy and concentrated but we got through unscathed and landed safely at base at 23.00hrs. Of the 535 aircraft taking part in the raid only one Lancaster and one Mosquito were lost. However, we learned that a further twelve Lancs were lost on a raid on Heilbron which took place at the same time.

Another new Lanc, "Able 2" joined the Squadron and, on the 7th December, we took it up on an air test. It was a beautifully clear day and Robbie got it up to almost 30,000 feet at one point. Using my "Gee" I homed the Lanc over Bingley, my old home town, where we did an orbit or two whilst I wondered if my folks down below would see us. As we climbed again there was a magnificent view of South West Scotland, Wales, Ireland and the Lake District on that remarkably clear December day. For the next two weeks we were grounded again. The Squadron did manage to get a couple of ops in but, although we were on the battle order a couple of times, we found that ops were cancelled almost as soon as we had got out to dispersal. On Christmas Eve the Squadron suffered its first loss in over four months when Flying Officer Griffiths and his crew failed to return from ops on Cologne. It was just after Christmas that I heard with sorrow and dismay that my old buddy, Bert Thomas, had been killed when his 'plane crashed on take off for the same raid. For our crew December had been a month of false alarms of briefings and cancellations – the old 'cat and mouse' game.

For the Christmas period Poker and I had arranged to bring our wives over to Cleethorpes for a few days. We had, of course, got Robbie's approval – after all, he was the Flight Commander -and we devised a code whereby a simple 'phone call to the digs would get us haring back to Waltham if we should find ourselves on the battle order. On the 28th December all hell broke out over the Humber Estuary. Poker takes up the tale:

"Annie and I had been in bed for an hour or so when we were awakened by air raid sirens. After a while we heard the sound of aero engines approaching from over the sea – that curious throbbing sound made by German bombers – which was quickly followed by anti-aircraft fire. We jumped out of bed and went to the window, which overlooked the sea front, and had a grandstand view of the action. A few miles out to sea we could see streams of tracer shells going up into the sky accompanied by the flashes of explosions. Then we heard a new sound approaching the shore – a spluttering like demented motor cycles – flying bombs air launched by the Luftwaffe just off shore. Much to our relief the engines kept going and the flying bombs passed overhead for some other destination. The racket continued for over two hours until the All Clear went around 3.00 a.m. The following morning we arrived, rather bleary eyed, for breakfast and asked Freda and Art what they thought about the night's events. They looked at us in astonishment. We recounted what had happened and they could hardly believe it. They had slept through it all and hadn't heard a thing!"

The following morning, the 29th, we received a "coded" message from Robbie and dashed back to Waltham. We had told Annie and Freda that if there was an op laid on we would get Robbie to fly along the sea front before setting course so that they would know not to expect us back before the following morning. From our experience of the time lag between briefing and take off we told them to start looking out at 3.00p.m. In the event, we took off at 15.12 hours and were whizzing low over the boarding house at 15.20 or so giving them a farewell wave from the cockpit before setting course.

We joined another 300 Lancs for a night raid on the oil refineries at Gelsenkirchen. Once again we ran the gauntlet of Ruhr flak and searchlights and although the target was covered by cloud we bombed through sky markers, laid by P.F.F. Mosquitos, making sure that Mo got a good photograph. As we turned on the homeward leg, however, we were coned by searchlights and completely dazzled by the beams as they reflected off every surface inside the cockpit. Once again Robbie was equal to the occasion with a tremendous side slip to port followed by a steep diving turn until we reached the safety of darkness. Looking back Poker saw another Lanc caught in the beams and watched it trying to escape until it finally disappeared from view. The raid, apparently, was successful. Freda and Annie had counted the Lancs taking off from Waltham and counted them in again on their return. There was one missing. Amongst the crew was an old friend of Poker's from his Ceylon days. We later heard that the 'plane had been shot up over the target but had managed to force land behind our lines in France but, the final horror, it landed in a minefield. There were no survivors.

And so ended 1944. Seventeen ops in the log book and thirteen to go. On the ground the allied forces were poised to cross the Rhine on a broad front whilst the Russians were massing to cross the Oder. One could now say that the end of the war was in sight but Germany was still fiercely resisting. The big question was, "When?"

Chapter Ten

THE MUNICH TRIP

The New Year opened badly for the Squadron. On the 2nd January Poker's favourite Lanc, "'ell for Leather" was returned to the Squadron after a major overhaul. Flight Lieutenant Weatherall and his crew took her on a training flight and bombing practice when, inexplicably, it crashed in The Wash. Three days later the Squadron lost another crew on Hannover.

As described elsewhere the success or failure of an operation by main force would depend upon a whole range of factors. The same applies to individual aircraft and crews. I suppose all aircraft had their idiosyncracies and crews would freely discuss particular virtues and vices of particular aircraft amongst themselves. Thus, for example,"I see you're in "B Baker" tonight. I had loss of power on the port inner on my last trip but 'Flight' says it's O.K. now."However, such problems didn't worry us. We now had our own kite, "Jug and Bottle", which was almost brand new.

January 7th, 1945, dawned crisp and clear. It was one of those cold, clear, frosty winter days without a cloud in the sky and it was such a day when ops would almost certainly be laid on. As usual, Ronnie, Gibby, Poker, Monty and I cycled over to the Flight Office to meet up with Robbie and Mo and have a look at the battle order, if there was one. Sure enough, there we were: "A" Flight, Squadron Leader D. Robb, "J"."O.K. guys," said

Robbie, "I'll meet you at dispersal in half an hour to check out "Jug and Bottle." We cycled over and clambered into the 'plane. Each of us checked out our equipment as Robbie ran up the four Merlins. I checked my "Gee" and "H2S" and other instruments and found everything in order and when everybody was satisfied we climbed out of the 'plane and speculated on the target. Robbie might have known but he didn't let on and, so far, we hadn't heard what the fuel load was going to be. Nevertheless, all around the station, the usual routine of preparing for ops was swinging into operation and the tannoy regularly called the ground crews to their tasks. Armourers cycled over to the bomb dump to load up trolleys with cookies and incendiaries; fitters and electricians crawled over Lancs performing last minute checks and adjustments. As the first tanker drivers drove their bowsers to the dispersals it was Ronnie, as usual, who was first with the 'gen':

"It's full tanks lads. Twenty one fifty four gallons. It's going to be a long one!"

Shortly after lunch navigators were called to the navigation briefing when they would be the first to learn of the target for the night and then draw up their flight plans based on forecast Met reports and wind velocities. There was always speculation before the actual briefing as to what the target would be and as we entered the nav section all eyes automatically focussed on the huge wall map at the front of the room. On the map was pinned a red tape which led from Grimsby, down to Reading and then to Beachy Head. From there was a long leg over France to a point near Saarbrucken and then a shorter leg to a point south west of Stuttgart where it turned east to Munich.

Standing in front of the map was our navigation leader, "Traff", or Flight Lieutenant Trafford:

"It's a long one tonight lads," he said, "so make sure you keep bang on track or you might find yourselves running out of fuel!"

Chalked on a blackboard at the front of the briefing room were the turning points, E.T.A.s and wind velocities for heights up to 20,000 feet. We collected our plotting charts and each navigator, individually, marked in the tracks to Munich and return. Then, with the aid of the Met and other information available, we calculated courses on our Dalton Navigational computors and drew up our flight plans cross checking with each other to ensure that we had not made any mistakes. The whole process probably took about forty five minutes after which we trooped out of the nav section to join the rest of the crews for main briefing.

This followed the usual pattern beginning with the Intelligence Officer describing the target and its importance which, in this case, were the factories in the industrial area of Munich. As he spoke Mo was carefully examining his target photograph and a topographical map of the approach to Munich.

"Going to have a go at the beer garden Mo?" I quipped.

"That bastard sure as hell wouldn't be in it if I did." he growled in reply.

The Met officer gave his briefing which included warnings of severe icing as we climbed through the cloud layer. We were briefed on the activities of Pathfinder Force who would mark the turning points, to concentrate the bomber stream, and the target itself. In an effort to confuse the enemy and dilute his defences diversionary raids would be made by Mosquitos to Hannover, Nurenburg and Hanau. Stress was again laid on the long distances involved and the need for accurate navigation – not only from the fuel point of view but also because of the heavily defended areas of Saarbrucken, Karlsruhe and Stuttgart which lay close to our route. In the event of delays in taxying out before take off bowsers would be standing by to top up fuel tanks.

The briefing had given us plenty to think about and as we went out to collect our 'chutes, flying rations and escape kits the talk and banter was more subdued than usual. Although our Lanc would not even be scratched and none of us injured this was to be the most gruelling operation of the tour being airborne for over nine hours from take off to landing. From my point of view it was to be the worst and most exhausting both mentally and physically but it was also a classic illustration of the skill and expertise of every single member of the crew. As we shall see, each, in his own way, contributed that special something which exemplifies the unique character of a bomber crew working as a team.

We were briefed to fly out at 18|20,000 feet and descend to 12,000 feet for the bombing run. Usually, after take off, we would climb to operational height over base and then set course but on this occasion, to conserve fuel, we were to climb on course to reach operational height over the south of England. We joined the queue of Lancs taxying around the perimeter track to the runway. Ronnie stood in the astro dome watching the flight controller and, as we took up position at the end of the runway, he called:

"O.K. Skipper you've got a green!"

With the brakes on Robbie revved up the Merlins until the Lanc vibrated as though it was going to fall apart. Then, with the brakes released, "Jug and Bottle" started to roll down the runway. Poker called out the airspeed as Robbie held her straight on the runway and then called out:

"Through the gate!" Poker advanced the throttles to maximum power and, after a few more seconds, Robbie lifted her off the ground.

"Undercarriage up!"

"Undercarriage up!" confirmed Poker.

My first log entry read: '18.20 hrs. Airborne.' We made a circuit of the airfield and I gave Robbie our first course. Two or three minutes later we started to climb on course for Reading which was our rendezvous point with another 644 Lancasters.

Six minutes after setting course I took my first Gee fix. It placed us a couple of miles port of track but it was too early to think of course alterations at this stage because the stronger winds at higher altitudes would swing us back to starboard. Around us were the rest of the Squadron and, in the distance, we could see dozens of Lancs from other squadrons in the Group. We now settled down to the long haul ahead. I took another look at my flight plan and compared the forecast wind velocity with the one I had obtained from my last fix and, finding little or no discrepancy prepared to take my next fix. Just as I was lining up the 'blips' on the time base they disappeared in a green fuzz, rather like 'snow' on a television screen. I checked the leads to the set and tried alternative channels only to come up with the same result. This was serious because, without Gee, it would be almost impossible to navigate with the degree of accuracy described above. Nor could I use H2S just yet because its signals could be picked up by the enemy and put the whole bomber force at risk. Again I checked everything but with the same result.

"Navigator to Skipper."

"Yes Art?"

"Sorry Skipper but the Gee's U|S. I think we'll have to go back." There a was pause. To this day I don't know what went through Robbie's mind. Only recently did I discover that during that pause Robbie and Poker were carrying on some sort of conversation in sign language consisting of pointing ahead, pointing back, gesturing with open hands and a thumbs up sign. From the outset it looked like being a rough trip. Munich was a long way off, almost 900 miles on the flight plan route and then we had to get back. Maybe Groupie's parting words had come to mind:

"Good luck! Good bombing! And NO EARLY RETURNS!"

"Well Art," came Robbie's voice over the intercom, "Look, I can still see some of the others so I guess we can follow them for a while. Wha'd'ya think?"

I was reminded of the American pilot of a B 17 'Flying Fortress' chatting to a Lancaster skipper:

"Y'know, I can't figure out how you guys can fly your missions at night without crashing into each other." He went on, "Oh Gee! I guess you keep your navigation lights on!"

I didn't tell Robbie what I thought of that. We had taken off at 18.20 Double British Summer Time and the sky was rapidly darkening. In my opinion it was very dodgy relying on visual contact with the others; it would be at least two hours before we could safely use H2S during which time we could stray a long way off track. I made these points to Robbie who thought about it for a moment or two and then:

"O.K. Art, I think we'll give it a shot. Let's press on a bit and see how she goes."

Still very unsure about it all I acknowledged. After all, Robbie was the skipper. Engrossed in trying to get the Gee set working and checking and rechecking my air plot I had missed a conversation between Poker and Robbie. Apparently the starboard inner motor had developed a fault and, instead of putting out its 1400 horse power, the prop was just 'windmilling'. Poker tried all he knew but with no success. This, of course, could affect our airspeed and rate of climb which, again, could add to the navigational problems. On the other hand the other three engines would take up a lot of the strain and Poker adjusted them accordingly. With hindsight I realised that the duff motor was also the cause of my Gee problem because the generator on that motor provided the power for my set. As we crossed the French coast "Jug and Bottle" had struggled up to 14,000 feet, well below our intended 20,000. Mo, who had been map reading down in the nose, gave me a pin point as we crossed the coast so I had at least one fix to work from so that I could calculate a new wind velocity and revise my E.T.A.

"Rear gunner to Skipper!"

"Yes Gibby?"

"Hey Skip, I don't think I'm getting any oxygen."

This was a new problem. I have already described the effects of oxygen lack but an additional effect was a feeling of cold. Even with his electrically heated flying kit Gibby would have felt the cold in the particularly low January temperature of – 40 isolated, as he was, in the rear turret.

"Look Gibby, we'll level off at this height and see how you make out. Meanwhile Poker will check the supply."

Poker turned up the supply to maximum but Gibby still wasn't getting any. Collecting an emergency oxygen bottle Poker crawled down the fuselage checking each oxygen point in turn but failed to find any fault.Leaving Gibby two oxygen bottles, each of which held about ten minutes supply, Poker made his way back to his position alongside Robbie who decided to take the Lanc down to 12,000 feet which should ease Gibby's problem.

For some time we had been well below main force and all visual contact was lost. Using the forecast winds and the fix Mo had given me I navigated on dead reckoning until I felt it would be safe to use the H2S. I studied the screen and chart for a while but was unable to recognise a definite ground feature but, just then, Mo's voice boomed over the intercom:

"Hey Art! I think we're O.K. I can see the flak from Karlsruhe and Stuttgart to port.Some stupid sonofabitch has strayed over there and woken them up!"

If Mo was right we were not too far off track but I thought it was one hell of a way to establish our position from two of the most heavily defended cities on the route! For a few more minutes I made more calculations and then gave Robbie a new course, almost due east, for the run up to Munich. We had barely settled on the new course when I got my first real fix of the flight. On the H2S screen was a dark, elongated sausage shaped patch with varying blobs of light around its edges – Lake Constance – Boden See! I got a bearing and distance on a town on the northern shore, Uberlingen and, to my amazement and relief, I found I was only twelve miles south of track. However, we were also twelve minutes early. As we were only about 90 miles from Munich it was going to be difficult to lose those twelve minutes. The usual way was to fly a series of 'dog legs', a sort of zig zag course. We could, of course, have done a little diversion over Lake Constance but this would have taken us further away from the main force and made us a more likely prey for night fighters. It would be better to creep back into the bomber stream which was a few miles north on our port side.

I instructed Robbie to alter course about ten degrees to port, got another fix and calculated my first reliable wind in almost 900 miles. The wind had veered from north west to north east and increased in speed from about thirty knots to over ninety! Although I could hardly believe this it did account for our early running and for being south of track. In any case, it was the best wind I had and I gave it to Mo to feed in to his bomb sight. Talking to other navigators, many years later,I heard of similar cases where the forecast winds differed so wildly from actual calculated wind velocities. Like me, they didn't believe it either!

Robbie decided to try to climb up to our bombing height of 16,000 feet and warned Gibby to use the oxygen bottles. I gave another minor alteration of course and then sat glued to the H2S set literally begging Munich to come up on the P.P.I when we would be about thirty miles away. Robbie called Ronnie up to the astro dome to look out for fighters- the rest of the crew were already searching the skies for fighters and the rest of the main force concentrating into the 'funnel' for the bombing run on Munich. The minutes seemed like hours. An irregular shaped blob of light appeared on the range finder ring of the H2S. I checked and checked again:

"Navigator to Skipper! Target dead ahead! E.T.A. ten minutes!"

The climb from 9,000 feet had reduced our airspeed a little

and this, with the, now adverse wind had reduced our ground speed but it still looked as though we would bomb early. Robbie, Mo and Poker searched ahead for the target and then Mo, with a hint of suppressed excitement called:

"There she is!"

There was still a few minutes to go."Got it!" called Robbie. "O.K. you guys, keep your eyes peeled!"

I started to fix up my P.P.I camera and confirmed the wind velocity for Mo – still over 90 knots.

"Hey Art, come up and have a look at this!"

I stood in the cockpit between Robbie and Poker and looked ahead, Although my eyes had not adjusted to the night sky, ahead and below I could see dozens of flashes and explosions lighting the scene. On the ground were countless fires interspersed with the red and yellow flashes of further explosions until the fires seemed to merge into each other like molten steel pouring from a blast furnace. Even today, after all those years, Robbie still laughs at my reaction:

"Bloody hell!" I said, and returned to my H2S.

Mo started to line up "Jug and Bottle" for his bombing run:

"Bomb doors open!" came that deep, deliberate drawl."

"Bomb doors open." acknowledged Robbie."Look out Skipper!" came a yell from Poker. Coming directly towards us was a Junkers 88. Robbie threw the Lanc down to port and, in the same instant, the 88 shot under our starboard wing. Poker, later, described the 88's pilot's face as white with his eyes staring in horror as he faced certain death in a head on collision with our Lanc. In a split second he disappeared fifteen feet below our starboard wing. But for Robbie's instant action neither we nor the Luftwaffe pilot would have survived to tell the tale. The corkscrew, of course, had fouled up Mo's bombing run so Robbie decided to do an orbit of the city and try again. In this he was enthusiastically supported by Mo:

"What's the point in carting this lot all this way to drop

them in a goddam field? You put 'em where it hurts the bastards!"

I mentioned earlier that I found time for a quick prayer over the target – this time I got two in! "How keen can one get?" I thought. "One doesn't orbit places like Munich with all hell breaking out below!" However, I kept these thoughts to myself -this is what was known as "pressing on regardless" and, of course, Mo was right. After the cock up of the flight out it was more necessary than ever to make a proper job of it.

During the hassle of the previous few minutes the bomb doors had been closed and we edged back into the bomber stream on much the same heading as before and, once again, Mo took over for the bombing run. Now, cold and calculating, he drawled:

"Bomb doors open!" Robbie acknowledged.

"Right . . . Right . . . Way over Right goddam it! Steady . . . Ste . . . a . . . dy" It seemed an eternity. To myself I muttered, "For Christ's sake Mo hurry up and let's get the hell out of here." But Mo was not going to be rushed:

"Steady, Ste . . . a . . . dy . . . Bombs gone!" Bomb doors closed!"Almost simultaneously with Robbie's "Bomb doors closed, "Robbie flung the Lanc into a dive to port to turn on to the new course out of the target area. Just as he levelled out a stream of tracers shot over the canopy and Robbie dived at full throttle into the cloud below. Over the intercom he shouted:

"Poker! The throttles!" Poker looked across to see Robbie hauling back on the stick but to no avail. He instantly closed the throttles and, between them, they gradually got "Jug and Bottle" back on to an even keel. In the dive the air speed indicator had gone right off the clock which meant the airspeed was over 400 knots. With the following wind we must have had a ground speed of 500 knots which is over 550mph. Not bad for a Lanc!

Now, back at cruising speed at 11,000 feet in thick cloud, Robbie called up the gunners:

"What the hell happened there gunners?"

"I saw a jet fighter in front of us so I had a go at him." called Monty, the mid upper.

"Well, in future let's know what's happening before you start pooping off Monty. You scared the shit out of us up here! Right, Poker, let's get up out of this bloody cloud!" Poker put on climbing power and we broke cloud at 14,000 feet. During all this we had been flying well port of track and I was busy working out a new course to rejoin the stream. We had been heading south west towards Switzerland, somewhere in the region of Ober Ammergau where the land rose to 6,500 feet and, a little further away, to 10,000 feet.

"Corkscrew port GO!" yelled Gibby from the rear turret, "It's there again!" Down we went again into the cloud and I warned of high ground. Then I found the H2S had packed in and we could have been anywhere within a radius of fifty miles or so. Gingerly, Robbie started to bring her up again when we heard rattles and bangings against the side of the fuselage.

"It's icing Skipper!" yelled Poker, "It's being thrown off the props. We'll have to go up again!" Once more we broke cloud at 14,000 feet. At some point in all this activity Gibby had warned of searchlights to port pointing vertically upwards. They were Swiss! Then, like fingers of light, they pointed repeatedly north towards Germany!

As we broke cloud Gibby again yelled:

"It's still there!" and down we went again. By now I was getting suspicious. Once more I warned of high ground:

"Navigator to Skipper. We'll have to climb or we're going to fly into the bloody Alps!" I had heard of these new jets but gathered that they had an operational range of only about twenty minutes. Of course, it could have been another one although we didn't think about that at the time. I finally persuaded Robbie to take us up again and left my table to stand in the astro dome.

"Where is it Gibby?" I asked.

"Way over there on the port quarter," he replied. I turned my

141

head to a point above the port fin and rudder. Sure enough there was a tiny, brilliant white light shining. In that clear, January night sky I saw the planet Venus as I'd never seen it before! Absolutely brilliant!

"It's bloody Venus!" I growled and, muttering foul imprecations to myself, returned to my table to try to figure out where the hell we were. Although nobody said anything I have the feeling that the rest of the crew were still a bit doubtful as to whether I was right and Gibby and Monty kept an eye on it until they were reassured!

"O.K. guys," called out Robbie, "let's settle down. Poker, will you take Gibby another oxygen bottle?" Ronnie chimed in:"I'll take it Skipper, I have one here and I'm the nearest anyway."

For my part I had the same navigation problems that I'd had on the way out but I no longer had H2S to fall back on. I fiddled about with it for a while but couldn't get any significant ground returns. I had set the air position indicator at Munich so I knew, at least, where we were assuming there was no wind! Using the last wind I had calculated I laid off a vector on the chart and calculated a dead reckoning position somewhere over the Vosges, thirty or forty miles south west of Strasbourg. We were about 550 miles from home and had no idea where the main force was by now so, for all practical purposes, we were on our own. However, we seemed to be fairly near the flight plan track so I gave Robbie a course which would take us to the French coast over 300 miles away. What I really needed was a couple of good fixes but as we were over cloud Mo couldn't pick up any ground features to give me a pin point; the Gee and H2S were out of action and loop, or radio, bearings wouldn't be too reliable at that distance. Ronnie did, in fact, try to get me a loop bearing but the quality was poor. I was left with astro.

I unpacked my sextant and looked up the tables for three likely stars or planets. Venus, of course, was bright and clear but too low in the sky for an accurate shot (No pun intended Gibby and Monty!) To take an astro shot in the air was a very tricky business. First, one selected a star and set its approximate altitude on the sextant view finder which was about as big as a postage stamp. Across the view finder was a horizontal line which was the horizon and, by moving the sextant fractionally, a bubble would appear. The trick was to get the bubble on the line and the star in the bubble. When the trigger was pressed the sextant would automatically take about sixty shots whilst the navigator kept the star in the bubble, dead centre, on the line. Of course, it was vital that the skipper kept the 'plane dead straight and level whilst the shots were being taken. As the first and last shots were taken the time had to be recorded to the exact second.

I gave Ronnie my watch with instructions to write down my readings and to carefully note the times. Then I warned Robbie to hold the Lanc dead straight and level and not to move an inch up, down or sideways!

"O.K. Art," he said "but don't take too long about it."

It probably took a couple of minutes to take my first shot and then I looked for another suitable star. Robbie was getting impatient.

"Hold it Skip, won't be long." I said.

The whole process probably took about eight minutes during which time Robbie was "Chrissakin" everybody to look out for fighters. It took another few minutes to work out the position lines from my astro shots and tables but, eventually, I had a 'cocked hat' – a triangle of position lines – on the chart. We should be somewhere within that triangle. Unfortunately my triangle covered an area of 50|60 square miles! I cursed in disgust.

By this time we had been airborne for over six hours. My jaws ached from chewing gum and all of us were tired. We often took benzedrine tablets to keep us awake on long trips but even so it still seemed a long drag home. Somewhere around 01.30

hours I estimated that we should be over the Channel so I asked Ronnie to get me a couple of loop bearings. The signals were poor and the resultant fix was as bad as my astro fix. For the whole trip Gibby had been having a hard time of it in the rear turret and, when he heard Ronnie giving me the loop bearings, hopefully asked for our E.T.A. base. Of course, I gave him and the rest of the crew the best estimate I had but, in the event, it turned out we were further south than I had thought. I left my table to stretch my legs and had a look through the astro dome. Above, was a clear sparkling starlit sky and, below, unbroken cloud. The Merlins droned on and on and there was a strange feeling of disembodiment alone, as we were, with little or no sense of motion. I returned to my table and had another go at checking our position and reckoned we had about 150 miles to go but felt that I had to have some confirmation of the course to fly.

"Navigator to Skipper. Is it O.K. for Ronnie to get me a Q.D.M.?"

"Sure Art. Go ahead."

This involved Ronnie calling up base and holding down his Morse key so that the operator at base could take a bearing on the 'plane. Ronnie went ahead and got me a Class 3 bearing which meant that the resultant course plotted could be up to fifteen degrees out. At that distance we could still be thirty miles or so from where we wanted to be on E.T.A. However, we made a small alteration of course and flew along for a while with each minute seeming like an hour. When I figured we were within fifty miles of base I requested another Q.D.M. and this was much better and we altered course accordingly descending slowly through the cloud. A few minutes later Robbie called up base on the R.T.

"Calling Nametab. This is J Jig. Are you receiving? Over."

Base responded immediately and gave us the cloud base and barometric pressure which we set on the altimeters. Keeping

144

out to the east Robbie broke cloud over the North Sea and, turning west, quickly identified the "GY" light on the ground. The runway lights were on and we received permission to go straight in and land. Nine hours and fourteen minutes after take off we touched down and taxied back to dispersal.

As we staggered out of "Jug and Bottle" we were greeted by the ground crew and a group of others including "Traff", the navigation leader. As I wearily trudged away from the 'plane to the crew bus, weighed down with my navigation bag, sextant and parachute he rushed up to me and grabbed my arm:

"Are you alright Chalkie? Have you been hit?" he asked anxiously.

Somewhat surprised at his questions I replied that I was O.K. but knackered.

"What about the others? Have you been shot up? Is the 'plane O.K.?"

Still wondering what this was all about I replied that we were all O.K.

"Then what the hell were you doing asking for Q.D.M.s?" he stormed. "There might have been someone badly shot up who needed Q.D.M.s more than you!" That did it. Tired out and depressed, at that moment I couldn't have cared less what happened.

"We should never have gone on the bloody op in the first place!" I bawled at him. "I'd no bloody Gee south of Nottingham, couldn't use H2S and we tried to play follow my leader all the f . . . ing way to Munich! Then the bloody H2S packed in. We just missed a head on collision with an 88, yo yoed up and down through the f . . . ing Alps and you ask me why I wanted two bloody Q.D.M.s! What the bloody hell would you have done?"

This was almost mutiny. I had recently been promoted to Flight Sergeant but Traff was a Flight Looey. I can't recall his reply but he must have been mollified. The crew bus took us back to debriefing where we recounted our exploits and, after rum, coffee and bacon and eggs we staggered off to bed.

The following morning I reported in to the navigation section and Traff grabbed me.

"Howdy! Are you in a better mood today Chalkie?"

Whilst I was in the nav section and, later, having a look at the P.P.I. photographs of the raid "Jug and Bottle" was being minutely checked over by the ground crew. According to the photographs Mo had chalked up another aiming point so we all cycled over to dispersal to see what the problem had been. The engines had been run up, generators, Gee and H2S checked, oxygen supply to rear turret checked and absolutely nothing could be found amiss. Poker wasn't satisfied and went to seek out the Flight Sergeant in charge of the ground crew. 'Chiefy' listened patiently as Poker recounted the night's happenings and then said:

"Listen, son, that kite's in perfect order. We couldn't find a single thing wrong with it. You must have had the bloody gremlins aboard last night!"

That was the last raid of the war on Munich and one of the most effective, Seven Lancasters – that's 105 aircrew – were lost.

Chapter Eleven

WINTER – PART TWO

The men who were lucky to live to see victory,
The men who went home to their jobs and their wives,
The men who can tell their grandchildren with pride
Of the bomber which helped to save millions of lives.

For the next three weeks things were pretty quiet for the crew of "Jug and Bottle" although the rest of the Squadron managed to get the odd op in. Somewhere around the 11th or 12th of the month a tall, cheerful looking Canadian skipper poked his head into our Nissen hut where Poker, Ronnie and I were lounging around having a natter. He was followed by three young sergeants and a flight sergeant. Grinning at us he said:

"Hiya fellers! We've just been posted here. Is it O.K. for my crew to bunk down in here with you?"

"Sure!" we all chimed up, sitting up and taking notice. One of us waved an arm round the hut and said:

"Take your pick."

"Great!" said the skipper, and then, to his crew, "O.K. guys, dump your gear and we'll go and grab some chow." Those were about the last words I heard from them because for the next two or three days they were on training flights whilst we did a bit of flying in "Able Mabel" on the 13th. On the 16th January the Squadron was briefed for an attack on the oil refineries at Zeitz.

Ten Lancasters were lost – one of them was Flight Lieutenant Quigley's. The following morning a sober faced officer and a couple of lads from the Orderly Room came into the hut and quietly removed all the young Canadians' possessions. We never even knew their names. In another few days a new, 'sprog' crew would arrive to take their places. Nobody said very much but such events cast a gloom over us all and, although the subject was never mentioned, the question of, "When would it be our turn," must have passed through many minds. Around this time another crew was lost. The Flight Engineer, Len Berger, was very popular in his section and had completed 97 ops. He liked to fly as 'spare bod' when a flight engineer was needed to make up a crew and aimed to do 100 operations. He was killed on his 98th.

On the 17th I did a 'spare bod' as navigator with Flying Officer Smith's crew who were detailed for a fighter affiliationn exercise and, a week later, we took "Y" Yoke on a bombing exercise – just to keep Mo's hand in. My nineteenth op came on the 28th when we were briefed for a night op on aircraft factories at the Bosch works at Stuttgart with a bomb load of high explosives. We took off at 18.35 hours in "Jug and Bottle" and this time she was as good as gold. Again we experienced heavy flak but got through unscathed arriving back at base at 01.30.

At some time in the month Robbie had advised me to put my papers in for a commission. The gunners had already done so as soon as they were nineteen years of age. Robbie hoped that all of us would be commissioned because, despite our unity as a crew, we still lived and dined in separate messes. Unfortunately, the powers that be were willing to consider the gunners and I but not Poker and Ronnie who were equally worthy and qualified. It was stressed that this was no reflection on Poker or Ronnie so maybe the R.A.F. was trying to economise. The R.C.A.F. was well heeled anyway! However, I filled in the papers which Robbie, as Flight Commander, passed without delay. The next step was to get the approval of the Squadron Commander, Wing Commander Hamilton.

February opened with another black day for the Squadron when Flight Lieutenant Conn and his crew failed to return from Ludwigshaven when another five Lancs were lost. On the 3rd February Robbie kindly loaned "Jug and Bottle" to the Wingco, who was on his second tour,for a night op on Bottrop in the Ruhr where the target was the oil refinery. The Wingco made up a crew of some of the section leaders including 'Ziggy' Zaggerman as bomb aimer and Vin Knight as flight engineer. I was to be navigator. I must say that I felt a bit overawed at the news because the theory that all ranks are equal in the air doesn't sound too realistic to a flight sergeant navigator with a Wing Commander skipper and a crew of Flight Looeys. However, we were called to briefing after lunch and took off at 16.15. We climbed to operational height and set course on the first leg. When we were nicely settled down I heard, over the intercom:

"Skipper to navigator. I want to get this over quickly. Give me a course direct to the target."

I was stunned.

"Navigator to Skipper," I called, "I'm sorry Sir but my orders are to proceed according to the flight plan."

There was a "Humph!" over the intercom. The Wingco had a reputation for being a bit liverish at times. I'd heard from a wireless op who once flew with him when he'd returned from an op in a bad temper. As they approached base the wireless op passed him the Q.F.E., (barometric pressure) to reset the altimeter.

"Blast •the Q.F.E!" he roared, "Let's get the bloody thing down!"

Needless to say, I felt I had to go pretty warily with this one and, without shooting a line, I can say that we stuck to track like a train on railway lines!

As was to be expected Bottrop, there in the middle of the

Ruhr, was very heavily defended. The flak was thick and heavy and Ziggy counted over 100 searchlights. Occasionally one would flash across the cabin but the Wingco weaved around in every direction and we never got coned. Whatever else one might say about him he could certainly throw a Lanc about. However, I gave Ziggy a nice wind for his bombsight and he seemed very satisfied with his bombing run. I gave Wingco a course for the first leg out of the target and, in a steep diving turn, he was on it in no time whilst I was scratching around the floor looking for my computor and 3H pencils. The rest of the flight was uneventful except that I noted Wingco had 'opened the taps'a bit and "Jug and Bottle" was going like the clappers for home. I didn't say anything this time because I knew he liked to be first back and Vin Knight wasn't as fussy as Poker about fuel consumption.

According to the reports it had been a very successful raid although eight Lancs were lost. Sadly, one of them was one of ours. Flight Lieutenant Ordell, a popular Australian, and his crew were lost. Charlie Scurr,their English flight engineer, was another of Poker's pals to go. After debriefing and bacon and eggs I got to bed around midnight and was awakened by the tannoy at 08.30.

"Flight Sergeant White to report to Wing Commander Hamilton immediately! Repeat, Immediately!" I shot out of bed.

"Oh hell what have I done now?"

I had a lightning shave, rubbed my shoes on the back of my trousers leg, jumped on my bike and sped to the Squadron Office. After straightening my tie and adjusting my cap I knocked on the door of the presence.

"Come in!"

I marched smartly forward, halted and saluted.

"Flight Sergeant White. You sent for me Sir."

"Ah! Yes Flight Sergeant. Hmm. That was a very good trip last night. You were quite right, you know, to stick to the flight plan."

150

"Thank you Sir."

"Now then. Ah – hmm – these commissioning papers. Yes, I think I can recommend you to the Group Captain. I'm sure you will make a good officer. Not let the side down you know?"

"Yes Sir. Thank you Sir."

"That's all then. Good morning Flight Sergeant."

"Thank you Sir. Good morning."

I saluted, made a smart about turn and marched out of the office. Phew!

Twelve days later I was detailed to fly as navigator with the Group Captain in his Oxford, a small twin engined job which was Groupie's 'runabout'. Ronnie came along as wireless operator. For some reason Groupie wanted to go to Southport so I went along to the 'flights' and the Met office to draw up a flight plan. On the way I met Robbie.

"Hey Skip, what's the cruising speed of these things?" He told me and I worked out a couple of courses but as the Oxford, unfortunately, didn't have Gee I would have to do some old fashioned navigating and I was a bit worried about the Met forecast of low cloud coming in. We took off at 15.30 and the flight was uneventful until our return when cloud base was down to 500 feet. Ronnie had been able to help with the navigation by getting me some bearings but, as mentioned earlier, they were nothing like as accurate as Gee. On E.T.A. base nothing but cloud was visible so I advised Groupie to fly east for another few minutes to break cloud over the sea. After a minute or two he asked:

"Are you sure we are over the sea now navigator?"

"Yes Sir," I replied, but you can go on for another minute or two if you want to be on the safe side.

"Yes navigator, I think I'll do that."

Ronnie had got the Q.F.E. from base so that the altimeter was set correctly so down we went through 2,000 feet of cloud and finally broke it over the waves of the North Sea at 500 feet.

Groupie turned west and put the Oxford down on the runway. The next morning I was called to his office. Groupie didn't waste any time:

"Now Flight Sergeant, about these papers" shuffling them around on his desk, "Your Flight Commander and Wing Commander Hamilton speak very highly of you so I have no hesitation in granting my approval." said he looking me straight in the eye.

"Th..Th Thank you Sir." I stammered.

"Don't forget, make sure you are over the sea before you break cloud!"

"No Sir! Thank you Sir!"

I did my best I.T.W. salute and marched out. That was it. I immediately collected a travel warrant and £50 worth of vouchers for my uniform and went on forty eight hours leave to get rigged up. On the 17th February I was officially discharged from the R.A.F. and commissioned on the 18th as 'Pilot Officer' (General Duties – Aircrew Category: Navigator) in the R.A.F.V.R on probation. When I arrived home I went to 'Brown Muff's' with my vouchers and two hours later collected my dress uniform, overcoat, flat cap, forage cap, shoes, socks, shirts, ties which I carted away in a new suitcase and holdall. There was time for a few pints with my family in the 'Mannville' and then it was back to Waltham. Somehow I had expected a day or two to get used to my new surroundings in the Officers Mess but I was unlucky because I found I was scheduled to take off with Flying Officer Burrell and his crew who were new to the Squadron and I was to give an H2S demonstration to his navigator, Sergeant Amey, on a cross country exercise. It was to be the following night before I was 'initiated', via a lot of beer, in the Mess, a pint of which found its way into my brand new flat cap. Once it was 'christened' Vin Knight nicked it and I was left with his. Actually, I didn't mind very much because his was more battered and 'had a lot more hours in' and it didn't look too bad once I had cleaned it up! I went through the ceremony of scratching my initials on Robbie's tankard and that was about it. Apart from that life didn't change very much except that Gibby, Monty and I now bunked down in the officers' quarters and I saw a bit more of Mo. On the other hand, the commissioning of Gibby, Monty and myself did seem to isolate Ronnie and Poker and I think they felt it. After all, we were the same team and had shared the same experiences – both good and bad. Otherwise the whole bunch of us still biked down to the locals as usual or got together in the social centre and the three new, 'sprog' officers spent as much time chatting with Poker and Ronnie in our old quarters as we had ever done.

THE PFORZHEIM RAID

Just to keep our hands in we did some local flying exercises in the new "'ell for Leather" on the 23rd and, the following day, we were briefed for a night attack on Pforzheim. The success of any bombing operation depended upon a whole range of factors which had to be taken into account when actually planning the raid. In order to inflict the maximum damage to a target the raid had to be concentrated into the shortest possible time thus swamping enemy defences and fire fighting services. Hence, as referred to earlier, accurate navigation and time keeping was essential. Then, flak and fighter defences had to be reckoned with and routes out to the target and back again were planned to avoid, as far as possible, heavily defended areas; diversionary raids were planned to draw off fighters; 100 Group despatched specially equipped aircraft to fox the German radio and radar systems; instructions to German fighters were jammed and, even, false instructions were given; German radar screens were jammed with "window".

Despite all the ingenuity of the tactics employed in the

planning and carrying out of an operation, however, things could still go wrong. The Met forecast could be wrong; forecast wind velocities could be way out; cloud and icing could foul things up. Perhaps the Germans were not taken in by the feints of a diversionary force; German fighter pilots might ignore dubious radio instructions and home in to a bomber's H2S; forecast ten tenths cloud might turn out to be perfectly clear – or the reverse.

It was the job of Pathfinder Force to identify the target. PFF Lancasters and Mosquitos would fly out a few minutes ahead of main force and drop flares, target indicators, red, yellow or green to mark the main rendezvous points, turning points and the target itself. If the aiming point was clear red or green ground markers would be used whilst another system of 'sky marking' would be employed if the target was obscured by cloud. In such cases Pathfinders would release 'sky markers' at a carefully calculated time and position so that the wind would carry the markers over the target area just as the first wave of the main bomber force was over the target. The bombers would then bomb the flares. In charge of the Pathfinder Force was the "master bomber". It was his task to ensure that the target was correctly identified and marked. As the raid progressed he would call up back up PFF crews to re-mark the target and instruct main force, over the R.T., to bomb accordingly.

The above is, perhaps, an over simplification of a very difficult and dangerous operation but it should serve to give some idea of the complexities involved in setting up a successful raid. When the outcome of a raid depended upon so many factors it is not surprising that there would be many varying degrees of success. In the case of the Nurenburg raid, when almost everything seemed to go wrong, 94 aircraft, that's 658 aircrew, were lost. Sometimes, however, everything went right and when it did it meant sheer devastation for the target city. Two such targets were Hamburg and Dresden and, even today, over fifty years later, controversy still rages over the rights and wrongs of those

154

operations. There is a third town, which never got into the history books, which suffered a similar fate. That town was Pforzheim.

Around lunchtime on the 23rd February, 1945, navigators were called to briefing. The target was Pforzheim. "Pforzheim? Where the bloody hell's Pforzheim?" "Never heard of it!" Pforzheim was an industrial town almost exactly half way between Stuttgart and Karlsruhe and, apparently, it specialised in making precision instruments for the German war machine. In fact, the object of the operation, according to our briefing, was to destroy the instrument factories.

At the time the Pforzheim raid did not strike me, nor anyone else I have spoken to, as a particularly memorable raid from the point of view of one filled with more than its fair share of incidents. True, it was a long trip – eight hours into the depths of Germany. We had visited Karlsruhe and Stuttgart before and had a healthy respect for their anti aircraft defences which would be thirteen or fourteen miles on either side of our track. The only reason that Pforzheim sticks in my mind after all these years is that it was the only target I ever saw when the target indicators were newly laid just prior to the actual bombing. It so happened that we were to open the attack but more of this later.

The sketch map of night operations on the night of 23|24 February gives a good illustration of the main and diversionary operations on that night. The Pathfinders flew, almost direct, from their Lincolnshire base sweeping just south of Strasburg to approach Pforzheim from the south west. 367 main force Lancasters from Nos. 1 and 6 Groups rendezvoused near Reading and crossed the coast at Beachy Head flying south east to a position just south of Paris. Main Force then altered course for a point near Nancy and then headed due east for the run up to Pforzheim. At the same time small, diversionary forces were heading for Frankfurt, Darmstadt and Worms whilst further radio counter operations were taking place over Northern Germany.

Pforzheim: Note Cascading T.I.s and 2 Lancs
Photo I.W.M.

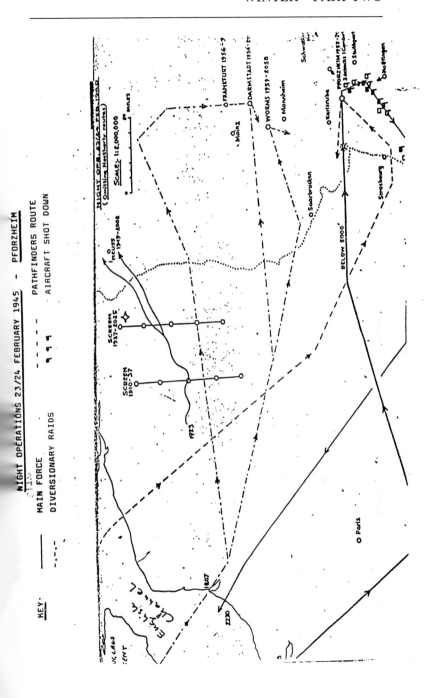

Not shown on this sketch was another raid by 80 Lancasters and Mosquitos on a "U" boat base on Oslo Fjord whilst yet another group of 70 Mosquitos was attacking Berlin.

Following the main crew briefing, which had been concluded, as usual, with the Station Commander's exhortation:"Good luck; Good bombing and no early returns," we trooped out to collect flying kit,'chutes, escape kit, flying rations and flasks of coffee and joined the transport to take us out to dispersal. Tonight we were flying in "M" Mike, a new aircraft on the Squadron, and took off at 15.55. We were carrying a bomb load of 1,000 pounders and were briefed to open the attack as PFF supporters. There was a lot of cloud about as we crossed the French coast which thickened appreciably as we carried on, south east, into Germany. Apart from that the outward flight was uneventful; the Met winds were reasonably accurate and only minor alterations of course were needed. We crossed the Rhine south east of Saarbrucken and, heading due east, we approached the target between Stuttgart and Karlsruhe with Mo laconically confirming our position from the flak bursts of those two cities.

Flying over unbroken cloud at our briefed height of 16,000 feet we heard the master bomber calling on the R.T.for us to drop to 12,000 amd then 8,000 feet to bring us below cloud. "Hey Art! Come up here and take a look at this! called Robbie over the intercom. As mentioned earlier navigators on my squadron were kept busy on the run up to the target by taking photographs of the P.P.I. tube and, consequently, got little opportunity to have a good look at the target. As Mo remarked to me when I met up with him in 1987:

"It was O.K. for you navigators, closed in behind your little curtain, you saw sweet F.A. of the action. If you had you'd have shit yourself!" Which, of course, was true! However, on this occasion, there was still a couple of minutes or so to the target before Mo would direct Robbie on the bombing run so I switched off my angle poise lamp and went up front to stand behind

Robbie and Poker. We were amongst the leaders of the attack and bombing had not yet started. It was a most peculiar feeling. Notwithstanding the roar of the Merlins it seemed, for an instant, that we were motionless – suspended in space and time. Ahead and below I saw a perfect circle of yellow flares ringing the town. Within seconds a cluster of green target indicators started to go down into the centre of the ring. It looked like Fairyland. There was no flak as yet but Ronnie, Poker, Monty and Gibby were searching the sky for fighters; with us and behind us were more than 360 Lancasters taking up position to drop their loads within that ring.

I can't remember what I said to Robbie over the intercom but my usual response when awestricken or lost for words in such a situation was "Bloody Hell!" or "Oh! My God!" Pforzheim was a sitting duck and Mo couldn't have a better target. I returned to my table and set up the camera as Mo took over the bombing run. "H" Hour was 20.00 hours precisely and, exactly on time, Mo opened the attack acting on the master bomber's orders to bomb the centre of the pattern of T.I.s. There was neither flak nor searchlights to be seen but as we crossed over the target we could feel the blast of our own bombs exploding which gave us a rough ride at that low level. With bomb doors closed Robbie opened the taps and put us in a tight turn to starboard and another starboard turn put us on the first leg home, south of Strasbourg, across France and back to base. We landed just before midnight and, after the usual debriefing, rum, coffee, bacon and eggs we went to bed and that was it – until a few years ago.

Early in 1985, as a result of an enquiry in "Airmail", I was contacted by a lady called Ursula Moessner, a History lecturer at the University of San Jose, California. Ursula was writing a thesis on the Pforzheim raid and had appealed, through "Airmail" for any ex aircrew who might be able to help her in her research and I was one of those who replied. We corresponded for about a year during which time I learned a lot more about the raid.

In the first place I discovered that the master bomber, Captain Edward Swales, D.F.C., a South African, was the brains behind the target marking I have described. Directing his back up markers, only 8,000 feet above Pforzheim, Captain Swales was attacked by an enemy fighter whilst we were actually bombing the target. The rear gun turret was put out of action and he lost two engines. Nevertheless he continued to direct the raid, which lasted twenty two minutes, until the end when he set course for home. The badly damaged Lancaster, hampered by turbulent cloud, was forced down lower and lower until he ordered his crew to bale out. His crew managed to escape but he, sadly, had left it too late and the Lancaster crashed and he was killed. Captain Swales was, posthumously, awarded the Victoria Cross and a plaque, bearing his citation, can be seen in the Bomber Command Museum at Hendon.

One other award for gallantry was won on the Pforzheim raid. After releasing its bomb load a Lancaster of 625 Squadron was hit by incendiaries from another Lancaster flying above – in much the same way as we had been hit at Emmerich – although the crew didn't turn out to be as lucky as we had been. Flight Sergeant Jack Bettany, the wireless operator, was standing in the astro dome spotting for enemy fighters when, looking up, he saw a monstrous shape appear right above him releasing its bomb load. Performing a fantastic feat of airmanship the skipper, Flying Officer Paige, managed to turn the 'plane away from the target area. Meanwhile, Jack, with his bare hands, managed to throw the burning incendiaries out of the 'plane. One of the starboard fuel tanks exploded and the starboard outer engine caught fire. The Skipper gave the order to bale out but the intercom had been destroyed so Flight Sergeant Bettany made his way through the fuselage to pass the order to the mid upper and rear gunners. Whilst doing this his 'chute caught on some burning debris, opened up and burst into flames. Nevertheless he warned the gunners and managed to clip on the spare 'chute.

The skipper was able to keep the 'plane flying until they were over France where they all baled out safely. Flight Sergeant Bettany was awarded the Conspicuous Gallantry Medal " . . . for his coolness, bravery and resolution in a critical situation setting an example of the highest standard."

From Ursula I also learned that, in addition to its importance as a precision instrument making centre, Pforzheim was also in the path of the advancing American armies and was an important centre of communications. Middlebrook and Everitt's statistics show that in this one and only raid of the war on the town by 367 Lancasters and thirteen Mosquitos 83% of the town was wiped out and 17,600 people died. Pforzheim came third, after Dresden and Hamburg for having the heaviest death toll of the war in one raid. Twelve Lancasters were lost on the raid and five other aircraft were lost on the diversionary raids that night. Sometime in the '60s the whole area was bulldozed away to form a huge mound outside the rebuilt town. It is known as "The Hill."

Ursula seemed impressed by my description of the yellow ring of markers. Before the war Pforzheim was the centre of the German jewellery industry specialising in custom gold jewellery. On official and business documents was the city symbol chosen by the city fathers. It was a gold ring.

By now we were the senior crew on the Squadron and, as such, were supposed to know all the answers. In December, 1984, Robbie came over from Canada to visit us. In one conversation he said:

You know, Art, you are one great guy but you did make one boob on the Squadron although it was partly my fault."

On the 28th February, 1945, we were briefed for a daylight attack on Neuss. This time we were to lead No. 1 Group. I have referred, earlier, to the "gaggle" and the plan was for us, in "M" Mike, to lead the "V" with the rest of the Squadron tagging on behind. We then had to fly to other points within a very short distance of each other where the other squadrons would form up into the gaggle when we would then head south to Reading on the first leg en route to Neuss. Needless to say, this was a very important and responsible role for us and, of course, the onus for the navigation fell on me.

We took off at 08.30 and circled base until everyone else was up and then set off for our first rendezvous just a few minutes away but when we arrived there wasn't a sign of the twenty or so Lancs that should have been hanging about. We turned for our next rendezvous and, again, the skies were deserted! We were obviously two or three minutes behind time and probably lost another minute or so on turns at the rendezvous points. At the same time I couldn't figure out where those minutes had got to.

"Well, Art, what do we do now?" queried Robbie.

Because of radio silence we couldn't call up base for instructions so I gave Robbie a course for Reading. Somewhere there were 180 Lancs heading south without their 'leaders'. I asked Robbie to increase the airspeed by ten knots, much to Poker's disgust because he liked to economise on fuel, and off we went to Reading. By now I had bitten my finger nails down to the first knuckle and then, dead ahead, we spied a whole bunch of Lancs heading south!

"Thank God," I gasped, All you've got to do now Skip is to overtake them and take up position a t the front."

We were just about to overtake the rear of the gaggle when Ronnie chimed in over the intercom:

"Message from base, Skipper, we're recalled to base."

Simultaneously 200 Lancs wheeled round and flew back home again!

Back at base there was hell to play. The shit had really hit the fan. My logs and chart were examined and I thought I was for the high jump. However, nothing happened and I never did figure out what had gone wrong until a long time afterwards. At the time Robbie said I had been given a wrong rendezvous and with that I had to be content. A long time afterwards the penny finally dropped. Sitting in my 'cabin', watching the second hand on my watch for the exact time to set course from base I naturally assumed that we were circling base. In the event we had drifted three or four miles downwind and that, plus the minute or two required to turn the Lanc round on to a new course, meant that we had actually set course about three minutes late. The blow was softened later when we heard that the target had been obscured anyway.

INTERLUDE

A prime requirement when being posted to a new unit was to "get organised". This meant, particularly in the case of the unmarried types, to make friends with a local family, landlord of a pub or find oneself a girl friend. Monty, for one didn't waste any time in doing this. Shortly after arriving at Waltham he became very friendly with a family who owned a farm adjoining the airfield and the family included a very attractive daughter. Naturally we would pull his leg about this but he took it all in good part maintaining that his interest lay in the wholesome food put before him in exchange for his assistance around the farm!

Mo, who was always a bit of a dark horse, was also very good at getting organised and seemed to spend a lot of his spare time in Grimsby or Cleethorpes. We found he had got himself a very classy girl friend but when we tried to draw him he just grinned and clammed up. Whoever she was he must have made an impression on her because, on more than one occasion, he came into my billet with a bottle of scotch with an enigmatic look on his face saying:

"Look, Art, at what somebody's bought me." In those days a bottle of scotch was like liquid gold. On one occasion he let it be known that he was going to date a particularly attractive W.A.A.F. R.T. operator. The poor lass had earned the nickname of "Jinxy Jean" because three previous boy friends had failed to return from ops and they were all in separate crews. When we heard the news we raised hell:

"You go out with her and you find yourself another bloody crew!" we roared. But Mo, as superstitious as any of the rest of us, had been winding us up to divert our attention from the real girl friend!

During our time at Waltham the Squadron had a large proportion of Canadian crews who had a tremendous effect on us, personally, and on the spirit of the Squadron. They were extroverts to a man, dedicated to the job in hand, tough and fiercely aggressive to the enemy. Yet, they had a tremendous zest for life. Off duty they were a crazy light hearted bunch getting up to all sorts of antics and showing very little reverence for authority. One day Ronnie and I were in the Flight Office. Ken Fraser and his buddy, Jack Playford had gone on leave to London and had given the Y.M.C.A. as their address. Jack Playford was the skipper of "Able Mabel" and, after completing his tour, he returned to take his old Lanc on its 100th op to Ludwigshaven. (Able Mabel" went on to complete 132 ops). However, on this particular morning Groupie came charging in to Robbie. He was furious. He waved a piece of paper under Robbie's nose shouting:

"See to this Robb! I'll see them when they get back!" Throwing the paper on the desk he stormed out of the office. It was a telegram addressed to the Officer Commanding R.A.F. Grimsby and the message read:

"Address now Regent's Palace. Grog's the shot, Gin's the gen. Love and kisses Jack and Ken." We roared with laughter as Robbie pinned it up on the notice board.

One Canadian, who I will call 'Joe', was the youngest pilot on the Squadron but that didn't stop him from getting into more scrapes than most. The first was at Hemswell, where we first met up, prior to joining the Squadron. Coming in to land Joe's Lanc overshot the runway ending up in a ploughed field. In fact he had allowed his bomb aimer to do a practice landing and, whilst the crash wagon was belting out towards them they switched positions and got away with it. On another occasion, after a particularly 'heavy' night, the crew was called for a daylight op at 04.00. Still feeling rough Ken, with the help of his crew, managed to make it through briefing and out to "C Charlie" and managed to take off. As soon as they were on the first leg he put 'George' in and promptly went to sleep being roused, periodically, by John Cooke, his Yorkshire flight engineer, for alterations of course and the bombing run. Poker recalls another occasion when, returning from a daylight op, we found ourselves flying alongside "C Charlie". John gave Poker a welcoming wave and Robbie edged over to port until we were flying almost wing tip to wing tip but slightly above. There was Joe, his head lolling back supported by his hands clasped behind his neck, hard and fast asleep, his feet propped up on the instrument panel flying on 'George' and oblivious to everything going on around him.

Like us, Joe had two Canadian gunners who were nicknamed Laurel and Hardy. The rear gunner was a tall, thin gangling individual with a shock of dark unruly hair crowning a rather cadaverous looking face. The mid upper, in contrast, was a short, plumpish lad sporting a walrus moustache, who always seemed to be reading a book. One evening, on the crew bus going out to dispersal, Poker was sitting next to him when the bus reached "C Charlie". Joe and crew got out but "Laurel" continued to read on. Poker nudged him:

"C Charlie – you're here."

"Aw shucks," he said, I'll go round again. I want to finish this chapter. There's plenty of time." Their looks and manner, however, belied their ability and dedication. They had a score of one enemy fighter shot down and one probable. Normally, if a crew saw another bomber under fighter attack it would get out of the area and step up its look out. When these two gunners, however, saw this happening they directed Joe towards and below the bomber being attacked homing in on the fighter's gun flashes and to get into position behind the fighter at very close range. The fighter would then get it from all six Brownings. John, the flight engineer, told Poker:

"They have a very belligerent attitude towards German night fighters believing in the theory that the more they shoot down now the less they'll have to worry about in the future!"

On another occasion on operations the navigator, deeply engrossed in plotting the course, was startled to feel a tap on his shoulder. Looking round he saw Joe, who should have been at the 'plane's controls, standing behind him.

"D'ya'know where we are?" asked Joe.

Another popular Canadian crew was Lyn Bell's. Lyn was a six ft. six Canadian from the Pacific Coast with his own particular brand of humour. "Doc" Watson, his bomb aimer recalled an incident when they were returning from a daylight operation on the Ruhr. Flying along in the "gaggle" they drew alongside an American formation of B. 17s returning from another raid. The Yanks, as always, were flying very professionally in strict formation whilst, to them, the Lancs appeared to be all over the sky. Edging his Lanc over to the nearest Flying Fortress he waved to its pilot and received a brief, almost curt, acknowledgement. Edging over a little more Lyn feathered the port outer engine and again signalled to the pilot and pointed to the idle props. He then feathered the starboard outer and again waved and signalled frantically to the Yank. Lyn's flight engineer, meanwhile, had stepped up the power to the other two engines keeping the Lanc on station with the B. 17. By now the Yank was beginning to look a bit anxious and Lyn feathered the port inner again pointing, in apparent desperation to the now, stationary three sets of props. The American now looked distinctly worried at this Lanc flying dead alongside on one engine when Lyn ordered his engineer to restart the three engines. With a final wave to the Yanks he opened the throttles and the Lanc raced away leaving the B.17 formation well behind.

Whilst we had very little contact with the Americans it was only natural that there should be a degree of rivalry. As ever, the Yanks always excelled on the public relations front which sometimes caused a bit of resentment amongst our crews. A case in point is the well publicised account, at the time, of the new, 'top secret' Norden bombsight, used by the U.S.A.A.F., reputed to be able "to hit a pickle barrel from 30,000 feet." The implication was that American bombs hit only factories, docks, marshalling yards and the like leaving everything else unscathed which was nonsense. As Mo and 'Doc' put it:"Sure, if they flew along singly in perfect conditions, they might be able to get a direct hit. But what's going to happen with a few hundred of them around, in strict formation, bobbing up and down and rocking in their own slipstreams? Add to that a box barrage of exploding flak – no chance! Neither could the goddam B.17 get up to 30,000 feet anyway!"

On the other hand not many R.A.F.crews would relish the idea of formation flying in daylight to targets deep inside Germany. The terrible losses inflicted on the U.S.A.A.F. on the Scheinfurt raids, for example, confirmed them in this belief. With the advent of long range fighter escorts, of course, the position changed for both air forces and, more and more, Lancasters and Halifaxes joined their American allies on 'daylights' whilst still maintaining the night offensive. As the Yanks would say, "We were all in there, pitching together," and we felt as bad at their losses as we did at our own.

American aircrew were amazed at a Lanc's bomb load. On one occasion a B. 17 crew, which had made an emergencey landing at Waltham, was watching the 'bombing up' of a Lancaster in preparation for ops that night. As the 'bomb train' of a 4,000lb. 'cookie' and 8,000lbs of incendiaries approached one crew member asked:

"Which 'planes are they going on?"

"This one." answered the skipper of the Lanc.

"No, I mean the rest of them."

"That's it. They're all going on this one."

Finally, "Doc" loves to tell the tale of the American crew that got lost. In parentheses I hasten to add that R.A.F. crews got lost as well! On one occasion a Lanc tried to land on Blackpool promenade! A wartime aid to all aircrew who were lost was to call up "Darkie" on the R.T. The procedure was for the skipper to call, "Hello Darkie, Hello Darkie." and then give his aircraft's recognition call sign when he would be given a course to fly to base or some other airfield. On this occasion a B.17 pilot called up "Darkie" but omitted to give his call sign. Again he called:

"Hello Darkie! Hello Darkie!"

He waited but there was complete silence on the R.T.

"Hello Darkie! Hello Darkie! Where in hell are you – you black- faced sonofabitch!"

Chapter Twelve

SPRING 1945

A beauteous, comely maid was she,
Her lovely form a joy to see;
She came as swiftly as the night
As graceful as a bird in flight
Into the green years of our life.
Not sweetheart true or loving wife
But dark, mysterious, proud, unknown,
To cherish, love, but never own.
Respectfully we learned to pay
Our tributes to her day by day
And as our lives with her entwined,
Our joys, our fears, our inner mind
Became a mutual living thing
To take upon our journeying.

("Ode to a Dark Lady." by Audrey Grealy.)

As the allied armies in the west gathered for the final onslaught into Germany Bomber Command and the U.S.A.A.F. stepped up daylight attacks on the Rhineland. In effect we were the airborne artillery blasting a path for the advancing forces and, as Field Marshall Montgomery wrote to Harris after the war had ended, "Your chaps made it easy for us."

March 1st dawned with a briefing for a daylight attack on Mannheim carrying fifteen 1,000 pounders. There was an escort of 400 Thunderbolts and Mustangs to sweep the skies ahead of enemy fighters and we never saw any, friend or foe. Take off was 11.30 and we arrived to find the target covered by cloud so bombed through sky markers and returned home without incident although three Lancs were shot down by flak. The following day I celebrated my 23rd birthday with another daylight, this time on Cologne. We were called at 03.00 for the navs meal and briefing and take off was 06.45. Again, we were after the communications system by attacking the railways with high explosives. As Middlebrook and Everitt put it, Cologne was now a front line city and, in fact, the Americans captured it four days later. We were briefed about the Pathfinders' role in marking the target and, as fine weather was expected, there would be no excuse for hitting the famous cathedral!

For a few minutes Mo and I sat together discussing the target:
    "Do you realise, Art." he growled, "that goddam cathedral has walls ten feet thick? It'll hold ten thousand of those Nazi bastards!"
    "I know how you feel," I replied, thinking of the father and the brother he had lost because of this war, "but the target is the railway yards."
    We took off at 06.45 and began the approach to Cologne, without incident, on E.T.A. For the past few months there had been reports, or rumours, on daylight raids of a new German anti aircraft weapon called "Scarecrow". The story went that this was a new kind of weapon which exploded throwing out vast amounts of black, oily smoke which simulated an exploding bomber. The idea, it seems, was that the sight of these explosions would deter crews from pressing home their attack on the target. Germany has always been adamant that such a weapon never existed.

170

*Three Waltham Lancasters leading a Gaggle From a painting
by G. Wragg* (Winnipeg Air Museum)

Poker describes seeing Cologne from a great distance away on this beautiful, sunny morning, 'nestling on the west bank of the Rhine looking so peaceful as we bore down upon it and thinking those poor sods are going to get a very rude awakening in a few minutes time.' "We began the run in, on the bottom layer as always, and I was keeping a wary eye on the aircraft above. We'd had one experience of being bombed by friendly aircraft and didn't relish another – especially as these were carrying 1,000 lb. high explosives! Just after 'Bomb doors open!' I spotted this Lanc about 500 feet above us and fifty yards or so ahead to starboard with his bomb doors open.I could plainly see the 1,000 pounders on the bomb racks and he was drifting ominously to port whilst we were slowly gaining on him. I immediately warned Robbie but we were hemmed in on each side by more Lancs and we just couldn't get out of the way. However, the words were hardly out of my mouth when the offending Lanc disappeared completely in a huge explosion leaving a great black cloud of smoke. Countless pieces of debris clattered against the fuselage whilst an undercarriage leg and wheel spiralled down to earth. This seemed to be the only piece left of a Lancaster, with seven young lads like ourselves aboard which, seconds earlier, was posing such a threat to us on its bombing run. The blast from the explosion threw us into a violent side slip to the accompaniment of a string of choice oaths from Mo, whose own bombing run had been fouled up, and acrid fumes permeated the cockpit. The Lancs on either side of us had dived away from us to avoid the falling debris and Robbie lined up "Jug and Bottle" again for Mo to have another run at the target. No sooner were the bomb doors open when another Lanc came drifting over towards us. 'There's another Lanc coming over us Skipper!' I yelled to Robbie and pointed towards it.'

"Let 'em go NOW! Mo!" bawled Robbie, "and let's get the hell out of here!" Mo pressed the tit and we got out of there – real fast!

Forty years later, when I met up with Poker again, we discussed this incident. It seems that, shortly after the raid, he and Annie saw a newsreel. The newsreel showed part of the Cologne Raid and, amongst the shots, was one of this explosion with four or five Lancs below it.

"That's us – underneath!" exclaimed Poker to Annie.

By another strange set of coincidences I was able to borrow the excerpt from the the film archives of the Imperial War Museum and Poker and I ran it through several times holding the frame at the relevant point. On the 'phone the Imperial War Museum had mentioned that the excerpt showed a 'scarecrow'.

"Scarecrow be damned!" snorted Poker as he watched the film. "That was a bloody Lanc and I had been watching it like a hawk until it disintegrated right in front before my eyes. Half the bloody undercarriage fell just in front of us and it's a miracle it didn't hit us. That Lanc got a direct hit but whether from flak or another aircraft above I don't know. One thing's for sure – it wasn't a bloody scarecrow!"

During the next week we did some more bombing and gunnery practice and, on the 12th, we were briefed for another daylight on Dortmund with take off at 12.57 in 'Jug and Bottle'. The raid was almost routine except that it was the biggest raid of the war with 1108 heavy bombers taking part. Just two Lancs were lost. Sadly, the Squadron lost Flying Officer Vale and his crew on a particularly nasty raid on Nurenburg when twenty four Lancs, 10% of the No. 1 Group force, were lost. A few days later, on the 19th, we joined 275 other Lancs for a night attack on Hanau. Again, there was little opposition to report and Hanau was accurately bombed. Fifty factories and over 2,000 houses were destroyed with over 2,000 casualties. One Lancaster was lost. (Middlebrook and Everitt.)

* * *

The 2nd April was a day to remember. A few days earlier we were informed that the Squadron was posted en masse to Elsham Wolds, near Brigg. The whole Squadron was going: Lancs, air and ground crews, stores, spares, bombs – the lot. All that would remain was a small maintenance party to look after the deserted station which was going to be used as a storage unit for "Manna" of which more, later. The news was greeted with dismay by most of us. Waltham was a happy station, we knew our way around and were well briefed on all the local pubs! At Elsham we would be sharing the station with 103 Squadron who were already well organised in the locality whereas we would have to start from scratch! We spent the morning packing up and getting last minute instructions about the move. Group Captain Newbiggin, our Station Commander, issued his last, moving, Station Bulletin ending with his famous words:

"Good luck! Good bombing and no early returns!"

A "2" had been painted after our aircraft letters so "Jug and Bottle" became "J2 – Jig 2" to distinguish us from the aircraft of 103 Squadron.

At the edge of the airfield was the farm where Monty had got himself organised and on this particular day there was a number of people standing around – someone said there was an auction – although I was never able to confirm this – maybe Monty had told them of the move and they wanted to wave us off. Whatever . . . they were about to see the finest air display ever – before or since! One by one the Lancasters of 100 Squadron took off to waves of "Goodbye" from those left behind. We, in "Able Mabel" took our place in the queue around the perimeter track until we reached the runway. As each 'plane took off it circled the airfield to make a little height and then, as if to a pre-arranged plan, it roared in at full throttle at low level to 'shoot up' the control tower with the wireless ops shooting off Very flares of every colour over the tower. The process was repeated by a couple of dozen Lancs as they made their

"Farewells" to the station that had been their home.

Twenty five minutes later the Squadron landed at Elsham Wolds and, after parking in the new dispersals, the crews made their way to their new billets. Mo, Gibby, Monty and I found ourselves in adjoining rooms in the wartime officers' quarters and we spent the next few days finding our way around and getting used to sharing the station with another squadron. We sampled the various pubs in Brigg and, one night, I had a rare night out with Mo when we went on his motor bike to Scunthorpe. The pub was crowded and Mo led me over to a group of three or four very sophisticated looking ladies who were sitting on the stairway which led to the pub's living quarters. I don't know what, if anything, Mo said to them but they didn't seem particularly interested in us so, after a couple of pints, we hopped on the bike and went back to Elsham. This innocuous little incident had a sequel two or three months later after I had left the Squadron. Waiting for a train at a little town somewhere in Leicestershire I found I had an hour or so to kill so I found my way to a little pub near the station. I ordered a pint and had another look at the lady behind the bar:

"Well, hello there," I said, "didn't we meet a while ago at a pub (I forget the name) in Scunthorpe?" She turned as red as a beetroot.

"Oh no," she said, "you must be mistaken."

"I don't think so, "I replied, "don't you remember that tall Canadian who came up to speak to you and your friends when you were sitting on the stairs?" She turned towards a door behind the bar and called to her husband who popped his head through:"Darling," she said, in a fluttery kind of voice, "this officer thinks he once met me in a pub in Scunthorpe but I've never been to Scunthorpe have I dear?"

But I still think she had!

It was at Elsham that I was first introduced to the game of Poker. I was very green and I had a lot to learn before I could out-bluff

Monty, Gibby and Mo – in fact I never did. After giving me up as hopeless dear old Mo wouldn't take my money from me!

Flying resumed on the 8th with a low level bombing exercise in "E (Take it) Easy". On the 13th we took off in "Jug and Bottle" for our one and only mining operation on Kiel Harbour. Mining was never really popular as we had to go in at seven to eight thousand feet and, of course, accuracy was essential. We had been briefed to drop the mines using H2S if the target area was covered with cloud and that is how it turned out to be. The great thing about H2S was that water showed up on the screen as a completely black area, bare land was a sort of greyish colour whilst built up areas showed as bright lights. Thus, by setting the dropping point in the range finder it was a fairly easy matter to 'home' the Lanc in on the target. For once, the run up was my responsibility and I gave the usual instructions for 'Bomb doors open' and talked Robbie in and released the parachute mines. With the bomb doors closed Robbie said he would stooge around for a minute or so, instead of tearing off back home as was the custom, to see if there were any explosions. If there were it would mean that the mines had hit the land instead of going into the harbour. In the event we didn't see any explosions so the mines must have gone where they were intended. As it happens there was another main force raid on Kiel on the same night where the target was the port area. For our sortie, however, there was a certain eeriness about it all flying, as we were, in thick cloud with no searchlights, fires or pathfinder flares to be seen – just the occasional burst of desultory flak. As we approached base on our return we found the weather had closed in and we were diverted to Wickenby returning to Elsham the next day.

On the 18th April we did our last real operation. It was a daylight raid on the naval base at Heligoland. It was a massive raid of, almost, a thousand aircraft directed against the naval base, airfield and the town. It was a perfectly clear day and the approaching bombers must have been seen, or, at any rate, heard from miles away. Poker described the sight of the wakes of hundreds of boats of all shapes and sizes leaving the island in all directions as the bombers approached:

"The wakes radiated out like the spokes of a bicycle wheel. There was every colour of smoke and flames from the explosions – even blue although I didn't see any green." Heligoland was, later, described as a 'crater pitted moonscape'.

The next few days were spent in preparing for "Operation Exodus" in which British prisoners of war, now liberated, were being flown home from Brussels. For some reason I never did an 'Exodus' trip although I took part in a practice. This involved doing a short air test and then landing to pick up a few ground crew as 'passengers' and taking off again for a short flight. We belted down the runway in "Jug and Bottle" for the air test when the port inner cut out before the wheels were hardly off the ground. The 'plane bounced over the road and hit a field twice before Robbie got her airborne. When we got back the ground crew had vanished!"

OPERATION MANNA

Throughout the war the people of Holland had suffered terrible deprivations under Nazi occupation and this was particularly true of Western Holland where the enemy held out to the end of the war. The winter of '44|'45 had been particularly severe and by early 1945 the people of Western Holland were literally starving. Treasured possessions, clothes, linen, blankets, anything of value were traded for a few kilos of potatoes; men, women and young children roamed the countryside on tyre - less bicycles looking for food of any description which would keep their families alive for another twenty four hours. People ate tulip and crocus bulbs and used all their ingenuity to make them more palatable. Some cooked them in engine oil. In those first months of 1945 repeated requests and pleas were made to the German military command for increased rations which were, nominally, at subsistence level but, in actual fact, were well below that but to no avail. In April, through the Dutch Government in exile, desperate pleas were made to Churchill, Roosevelt and Eisenhower and at last, towards the end of the month, a truce was arranged with the German Commander in Western Holland so that Bomber Command and the U.S.A.A.F. could drop food supplies in selected areas. The Germans made it a condition that the 'planes flew in at fifty feet until they reached the dropping area when the 'dropping run' would be made at 500 feet. On the face of it this was a very dodgy operation because the bombers would be sitting ducks for the German anti aircraft defences if the Germans broke their word.

Needless to say a lot of unease at these arrangements was expressed at briefing but orders were orders and it was a chance we had to take. On the other hand there was tremendous satisfaction amongst the crews at having the opportunity to fly on a, truly, mercy mission after the years of spreading devastation over Western Europe. "Operation Manna", "Bread from Heaven", caught the imagination of every crew that flew upon it. In addition to the packages of flour, dried egg, tinned meats, spam, tinned stew, biscuits, chocolate and countless other food items aircrew threw out their own flying rations of chocolates, chewing gum, boiled sweets and cigarettes that they had been accumulating. The first drops took place towards the end of April but it was much later when we heard how the Dutch first heard of the plan. The news had been broadcast by the B.B.C. and had been picked up by people squatting over illegal radios in upstairs rooms. As zero hour for the drop approached thousands of Dutch men, women and children thronged the streets and every available vantage point to search the skies to the west for their first sight of the bombers bringing food – instead of bombs.

On the 2nd May we took off in "M Mike 2" at 11.50 for the ninety minute flight over the North Sea to our dropping point near Rotterdam. Flight Lieutenant Vin Knight joined Poker and came along as spare flight engineer. It was an exhilerating experience skimming fifty feet over the North Sea at 150 knots. Crossing the Dutch coast we climbed to 500 feet and, looking down through the perspex bulge, Poker reported rifle bearing German soldiers on the flat roofs watching the procession of Lancs roaring in and as we turned for the dropping zone we just managed to clear a church steeple. On the ground were hundreds of Dutch people cheering and waving flags, handkerchiefs, even bed sheets as the Lancs came in low over their heads. The dropping zone was a patch of open country, just outside Rotterdam, and it had been marked by P.F.F. flares. It was here that Mo and I had our one and only disagreement. According to my briefing we went in at 500 feet whereas Mo was convinced it was 1,000 feet. There wasn't time to argue because we could only do one run over the dropping zone so Robbie took my word for it and we went in at 500. Forty years later Mo still remembered the incident and spoke to Monty about it and Monty passed his somewhat unsavoury comments on to me. When I finally met up with Mo again in '87 I think I was forgiven if, indeed, I was at fault.

"Y'know, Art," he said, "at 500 feet that aiming point was coming up pretty goddam fast!" He was the same old Mo, now 76 years of age.

"I know, Mo," I replied, "but I guess it doesn't matter now anyway. The Dutch still got their rations." The dropping of "Manna" was both a heart warming and a very moving experience but it also had its funny side later on when crews got to talking about it together.

"Did you see that sack of flour hit a cow?"

"Some stupid navigator must have taken 'em in on the wrong heading!"

The food supplies were supposed to be collected and stored in depots for allocation to the people by local Dutch authorities. In typical Yorkshire accents one rear gunner described, in sombre tones, an incident he saw:

"Art, all those foodstuffs we dropped were supposed to go into a warehouse to be shared out weren't they?"

"Yes." I replied.

"Well, when we went in we saw a feller on a bike with a bundle of stuff on his handle bars pedalling away like hell. Our mid upper was chucking stuff out of the side door and one of the bundles hit him and knocked him off his bike. It might've killed him might'nt it?"

"Getting clobbered with a bag of groceries at 200 knots could well do that." I answered.

"Well, I'd be very sorry if it did but it'd've been his own fault wouldn't it? He should have put it in the warehouse with the rest of the stuff."

Flying back over the North Sea Vin Kinight said to Robbie:

"Let's see how fast she will really go. Is that O.K. with you Poker?"

"Sure, go ahead," replied Poker, "You're the boss."

Robbie opened up "Mike's" four Merlins and we belted back home, down at fifty feet again, at something around 300 knots. We landed at 15.00 precisely and, as we turned off the runway on to the perimeter track we saw Ronnie standing by his bike bawling something to us. We taxied back to dispersal and, waiting for us was Ronnie who, for some reason, hadn't been with us on this trip. As we climbed out of the door he yelled:

"We're screened!"

Our tour of ops was officially over although most of us, apart from Robbie, were one or two short of the required thirty. On the other hand, we had run out of war although there was still the chance of being posted to "Tiger Force" which was being assembled for the war against Japan.

I cannot recall the blur of events that followed nor, it seems, can anybody else. Robbie thought we had gone out to dinner at the "Yarborough Hotel" whilst Poker thought we had a booze up in Brigg. Whatever we did, we had a party and it is pretty sure that we recounted our exploits together over the past seven months. We had our crew photograph taken in front of "Mike 2" in which we had done our last op and then it was packing up, form filling and preparations for going on end of tour leave the following day. I went down to the nav section with my gear and handed in my sextant, Douglas protractor, long plastic rule and Dalton computor. I was allowed to keep my Omega navigator's watch, which is the finest watch Omega ever made, until I was finally demobbed over a year later. On the 4th May, 1945, the seven of us met up together before going our own separate ways. The Canadians would be going back home whilst Poker, Ronnie and I would be split up and posted to other units. After eleven months as a member of a crew I suddenly felt a sense of loss. For seven months on the Squadron we had entered each operation in our log books watching the number laboriously climb to that magic "30" when we would be "screened". Now that it had come there was a sense of anticlimax. As Poker had said, "We were like family," and now, it seemed, we would never see each other again.

For me, those sentiments didn't strike me until the euphoria of end of tour leave faded. On that sunny May morning Ronnie, Poker and I amidst much back slapping, "Good Lucks!" and "Happy Landings!" made our farewells to those four Canadians with whom we'd shared so much. We slung our kit into the little 'Hillman' truck and climbed into the back for the short ride to the railway station. The W.A.A.F. driver engaged gear and we started off down the dusty road to the guard room.

Robbie, Mo, Monty and Gibby stood watching us and giving

us a final wave as we turned into the High Street and disappeared from sight. But for the amazing set of coincidences described at the beginning of this story we would never have met again. I shall never see Ronnie again but there remains that tenuous link with his son, Squadron Leader "Jim". Poker and I are still in regular contact but I last saw the Canadian bunch in '87 although we still keep in touch. Mo, now in his early 80s, is not so good with deteriorating eyesight and badly crippled arthritic fingers. I spoke to him on the 'phone yesterday but he wouldn't tell me much except that he wasn't feeling so good. When I tried to press him he growled, in much the same way as he did forty five years ago:

"You're asking a lot of questions aint you Art?"

"Sure," I replied, "but you aint answering them! I'm coming over to see you soon so I hope you're fit enough to make me a cup of coffee."

"Coffee?"

"Yes, coffee."

"O.K."

I'll be going when I've finished this.

Chapter Thirteen

LOOSE ENDS

> *She opened wide her arms to share*
> *With us the perils of the air.*
> *Her steadfast spirit, loyal, true,*
> *Was always with us as we flew.*
> *She never faltered, even though*
> *She might be wounded, weak and slow.*
> *We raise our glasses, drink a toast,*
> *Remembering a very host*
> *Of things that time cannot transcend,*
> *A gallant mistress, servant, friend,*
> *We loved her to the very end,*
> *My Lady Lancaster.*

(Ode To a Dark Lady. By: Audrey Grealy.)

This story wouldn't be complete without referring to another remarkable aspect of the flyers of Bomber Command – that strange affinity they had with their own, or one, particular aircraft irrespective of its type. The "Bomber Boys" had to have their bombers and some crews, having done a few ops in the same aircraft might begin to regard it as their own. They began to take a proprietary interest in it, so much so that they would be quite apprehensive if another crew should be detailed for their "kite" or they had to take another. Hence, skippers and crews became identified with particular aircraft. At briefings one would hear such remarks to skippers as:

"Dave, you're taking "H How" tonight."

"Oh, that's Henry Brown's kite. Is he on leave?"

Similarly, each aircraft had its own individuality – its vices and its virtues and each crew member would have his own loves and hates about it. Thus, for example, "L Love" had the best set of Merlins on the squadron. "D Dog's" radio was always on the blink; "V Victor's" Gee was u|s beyond three degrees east. Or, "They got "Able 2" up to 29,000 feet."

This personification of aircraft was carried to amazing lengths. Ground crews logged each op by painting a bomb on the fuselage below the cockpit. If its crew shot down an enemy fighter it was credited with a swastika. Excitement mounted on a squadron as an aircraft approached its hundredth operation and the take off on its 'century' was cheered by scores of airmen and airwomen of all ranks as they lined the runway shouting: "Good Luck!" and they would be back on the runway to greet it on its return. It is believed that about thirty Lancasters completed 100, or more ops. Commanding Officers even painted D.S.O.s and D.F.C.s on some of these veterans. Former aircrew still remember "old so and so taking "S Sugar" on her first op and Jack Playford coming back to take "Able Mabel" on her hundredth.

It is a sad fact that of the 7,000 Lancasters built during the war only two remain flying. There is our own "City of Lincoln" of the Battle of Britain Memorial Flight and the "Mynarski" Lancaster rebuilt in Canada by a group of dedicated enthusiasts and kept flying by voluntary donations. Scattered around airfields in Britain and the Commonwealth are a few more, that will never fly again, guarding the entrances to bases now flying jets. Of the few that we flew in "'ell for Leather" crashed mysteriously on a training flight, "K King" crashed on take off from Carnaby after a tyre burst and "F Fox" was lost on a raid on Ludwigshaven. The rest, Ken Fraser's "C Charlie", "Mike 2", "Love 2", "B Baker" and our own "Jug and Bottle" were ignominiously scrapped by 1946. The illustrious "Able Mabel" survived a little longer at Bomber Command Instructors' School but ultimately met her fate in September 1947.

No account of squadron life would be complete without some reference to its songs. Airmen were great singers and they really came into their own in the mess – especially when there was a 'stand down'. 'Tanked up' with a lot of beer they would roar out the squadron songs to the accompaniment of a battered old piano. Having exhausted their repertoire of squadron songs they would turn to "Sylvest" ("With a row of forty medals on his chest") or "Salome" which is unprintable! Parodies were made of popular songs of the time:

'A ride through London in a rattling taxi,
'With dirty noises from a horse's jacksie,
'A mattress without springs, those foolish things
'Remind me of you.'

And so, Ian, I think that is it! I think I have got all the bits that matter together although one or two disjointed pieces still stick in my mind – like the corny old line shoots:"There we were, upside down at zero feet with nothing on the clock but the maker's name – it was Smith!'

'That's strange, so were we but we were climbing!'

'Say Art, if you found yourself ten miles off track would you alter course to join the main stream as quickly as possible or would you simply alter course for the target?'

'Couldn't say, old boy, I never get off track!"

'Only fools and birds fly and birds don't fly at night!'

'Some stupid sod had left his R.T. switched on. A Junkers 88 came in and his rear gunner yelled:"Corkscrew port go!" and the whole bloody bomber stream corkscrewed!'

The briefing had been particularly sombre. The Intelligence Officer described the importance of the target and its heavy flak defences. Crews were warned of fighter airfields close to their route which took them near more heavily defended cities. The Met Officer warned of severe icing conditions and ten tenths cloud up to 20,000 feet. There was a danger of fog closing down base before the crews returned. The C.O. ended the briefing by re-emphasising the dangers and warned of the risk of collisions in the air. Finally:

"Any questions?"

There was deadly silence . . . , . . . and then a little Sergeant Airgunner stood up.

"About our escape kits Sir?"

"Yes Sergeant?"

"Is there enough foreign currency in them for us to have a bloody good piss up if we get shot down?"

As a Torpedo Bomber Squadron 100 Squadron served in the Far East flying the Vickers Vildebeest and was virtually wiped out by the Japanese at Singapore in 1942. The Squadron was reformed at Grimsby on the 15th December, 1942, flying Lancasters. In 3,984 sorties, 280 raids, the Squadron lost 92 aircraft and a further 21 in crashes. The Roll of Honour lists 592 aircrew who were killed.

Bordering the eastern boundary of the airfield, near Holton le Clay, is the A 16 Grimsby to Louth road. The short runway ends in a thin line of trees just a few yards from the road. Forty five years ago this road would be closed if the Squadron was using this runway. All traffic would be stopped as a couple of dozen fully laden Lancs took off – just skimming the tree tops with their undercarriages. Drivers of waiting cars and lorries and passengers in buses, deafened by the roar of Merlins at full throttle a few feet above their heads would wave and might even see an airman waving back. Perhaps they would wish the crew, "Good Luck!" Between the line of trees and the main road there is now a short access track to a small field. Here, there is a simple, granite memorial stone to 100 Squadron.

On Sunday, 15th September, 1985, the Squadron came back to Waltham again when forty or so airmen of the '40s gathered with their wives and friends for the short memorial service which ended the annual reunion of the Waltham Association. At

100 Squadron Memorial, Holton Le Clay.

Opening ceremony at 'The Jug & Bottle', Holten Le Clay.
Photo: Joshua Tetley & Son Ltd.

188

precisely 1.00 p.m. Wing Commander Mike Purdie, R.A.F.,
Officer Commanding 100 Squadron at R.A.F. Wyton, stepped
forward and laid a wreath on the memorial. As he raised his
right arm in salute a lone 100 Squadron Canberra flew overhead,
dipped its wings and disappeared behind the line of trees.

A couple of hundred yards or so, down the road from the
Squadron Memorial, stands an imposing new pub. Much of the
land which was RAF Waltham has been taken over for
development such as housing, light industry and, maybe, a golf
course. The pub was built by Joshua Tetley's Brewery on the
site where "Jug and Bottle" used to 'sit' at dispersal and so it is
only natural that the pub should be called "The Jug and Bottle".

In April, 1992, Robbie and Wally Nobes, who also flew the
'plane, joined Poker and I to officially open the new pub. It was
a happy, though nostalgic, occasion as the gathering of officials,
locals and we who had flown the 'plane raised our glasses in a
toast to our 593 absent friends who had failed to make it fifty
years ago.

The New 'Jug & Bottle',

POSTSCRIPT

That was supposed to be the end of the story but Ian, always the perfectionist, still wanted me to delve deeper into my thoughts to extract the last ounce of memories. After a gap of over forty years this isn't easy. However, as Robbie would say, "We'll give it a shot!"

The cohesion of a crew has been described and analysed countless times and I can think of no other group of seven men, so closely bound together, who came from such a wide range of backgrounds and yet retained their own individuality. In our case, a young Canadian from Winnipeg, who worked in an office concerned with wheat marketing, trained as a pilot and spent thousands of hours as an instructor before joining Bomber Command and becoming our skipper. In that time, through his skill and dedication, he was awarded the Air Force Cross to which was added the Distinguished Flying Cross for that same dedication and spirit as skipper of a Lancaster crew. Mo had worked in the timber industry in British Columbia before enlisting in the R.C.A.F. Tall, dark, with twinkling blue eyes set in a leathery, weather beaten face, he was the sort of guy we had read about in the "Rover" or "Wizard" when we were kids. He had worked in all branches of the timber business from lumberjack to mill manager. Because of his age he had great difficulty in being accepted for aircrew but, somehow, he managed to wangle it. Mo came top in his training courses and, probably, had the best record on the Squadron. Mo's was a private war. Germany owed him.

Gibby and Monty were both just over seventeen years old when they enlisted. Gibby was a lithe, fair haired young lad from a farming family in Innisfail, Alberta. Monty hailed from Ottawa and was rather stockier than Gibby. Monty, apparently, got some 'flak' from his Dad for enlisting so young but he carried on nevertheless. They had that keeness, aggressiveness and sense of adventure and daring deeds typical of their age. At eighteen they were air gunners in Lancasters and at nineteen they were commissioned officers in the R.C.A.F. with a tour of ops behind them.

To me, Poker was a veteran R.A.F. man already wearing the ribbon of the 1939|43 Star having served in the Far East as a fitter before being driven out by the Japanese. As a flight engineer he was first class and he knew the Lanc inside out and was, indeed, Robbie's right hand man. Despite his experiences in the Far East he had a boyish sense of humour and amused us all with his wisecracks tinged with dry Yorkshire wit. Before the war he had been an apprentice engineer, a career he returned to when the war was over. Ronnie, our wireless operator, had been a clerk at a colliery in Durham. He was a particularly conscientious member of the crew, always had his job 'buttoned up' and was always smartly turned out. He had a certain seriousness about him when on duty which rapidly disappeared to be replaced by typical Geordie humour. If a few of us were making a row in the hut it was Ronnie who would quietly remonstrate: "Hey! Where do you think you are? Home or some other dirty place?" It was Ronnie who always seemed to have an ear to the grape vine and was always up to date with the latest news of events on the Squadron and of the other squadrons in the Group.

Of the whole crew I suppose my life had been the most

sheltered. I had always had three or four close friends but lacked the gregariousness of the Canadians. I think I was rather naive – even gullible – and took authority more seriously than most. Each of us, during training, had been instilled with the importance of our position in a crew and how the lives of six others would depend upon our own individual actions. I suppose I took all this very seriously after crewing up. Could I meet the standards set by the others? Perhaps they felt the same way. I didn't know if I could meet these standards but I worked and practised at my navigation to be as sure as I could be that we got there and back on track and on time. I felt this most strongly on the Munich trip. Was I, after all, going to let them down but I've got to hand it to that bunch. They left it to Robbie and me to sort out and the only comment when we got back was: "That was a bloody long one!"

Socially, Monty, Gibby, Poker and I spent a lot of time together as N.C.O.s cycling to a pub, chatting over tea and buns in the social centre or just lounging around the billet when we were not down at the flights or working in our particular sections. Mo was the loner although we did have the occasional night out together. Robbie, as a Flight Lieutenant and, later, as Squadron Leader and Flight Commander was more involved with the section heads, commissioned skippers and other higher ranking officers in the Mess although, again, we went out as a crew pretty regularly when any barriers of rank disappeared.

It is difficult to describe my feelings on ops beyond those I have already outlined. Initially we were faced with a tour of thirty with the odds heavily stacked against us completing it although the odds improved tremendously in our favour both as we gained experience and as the war neared its end. I, for one, was one of those who felt 'it couldn't happen to me' but, at the same time, approached each one with a tense knot in my stomach until the pressure of work in my little 'cabin' made me forget it. This is one example where the value of training came in. Even the hours and hours of drill and marching in the early days had their value in instilling instant response to commands and altered situations. The months of plotting hypothetical flights on the ground and the putting of theory into practice in the air was to pay off on ops. For most of the flight it was a matter of constant plotting, fixing position, calculating courses and E.T.A.s. Having said that there was that initial 'gulp' and "Oh Hell!" at briefing when a particularly tough target was first revealed.

Through all this we worked together like clockwork . Robbie was the skipper who had to make the ultimate decisions and, at the end of the day, he was always right. He was a first class pilot who flew his Lanc every yard of 30,000 operational miles without the aid of 'George' and, as he once reminded me, he never did an overshoot in his life. I even learned to allow an extra degree on my courses to compensate for his tendency to put slightly more pressure on his left rudder!

Short of being shot up the worst thing that could happen to an airman was to go 'LMF' – to be accused of lack of moral fibre. Sadly, it happened that a flyer might feel he couldn't face any more operational flying. It could happen to any member of a crew at any stage. A pilot might 'find' an engine fault; navigation aids could go wrong; a radio could be repeatedly faulty; guns would jam and so on. When a crew aborted an operation two or three times for similar reasons that crew member was suspect. Apart from anything else he was a danger to the rest of the crew. It would reflect on the squadron's failure to provide 'maximum effort'. Such a crew member would be grounded pending an investigation and, if found to be LMF he was stripped of his rank and brevet and given the lowest job to be found until posted. In my view, although I never met such an unfortunate airman, this was the cruellest punishment meted out by the R.A.F. We had a lucky tour with just a few hair raising incidents but many a crew literally flew through flak and hell fire time and time again.

194

It was with a feeling of sadness and dismay that we learned of colleagues reported missing or killed. I can still picture those empty beds in our Nissen hut when F|Lt. Quigley and his crew failed to return from Zeitz. I was particularly shocked at the deaths of Sid Pick and Bert Thomas. Even today I still think about them a lot – two completely contrasting characters but good friends nevertheless. Sometimes, on the few occasions when I saw a target I was awestruck at the devastation we had helped to create but consoled myself with the thought that this was war. I remembered the German blitz; I remembered a young nurse bombed out of hospitals in London and Southampton only to be finally killed in an air raid on Glasgow. And so, as time passed, one became hardened – it was us or them. Those who have tried to discredit Bomber Command should look at war as it really is. Despite Hague and Geneva Conventions there are no rules of war – it's the aggressor who makes the rules. Hitler's rule was "Blitzkrieg" – "Total War". I, personally, have no regrets. As the quotation goes: "He who sows the wind shall reap the whirlwind." Bomber Command didn't do anything the Lufwaffe hadn't done – they simply did it better.

History is full of "Ifs". What would have happened, with Fighter Command down to its last reserves, if the Battle of Britain had lasted for another couple of weeks? What would have happened if Hitler had not invaded Russia when he did? What would have happened if Japan had not attacked Pearl Harbour and the Americans remained neutral? The answers are anybody's guess. One thing is certain. Without Bomber Command we would never have won the war.

Where are the "Bread and Butter Bomber Boys" today? Robbie, a widower and retired, lived near Toronto. He was an active social worker with the Canadian "Legion" and occasionally popped down to the Royal Canadian Military Institute to look up old wartime buddies. Turned seventy he, like most of us, suffered from creaking joints but still retained that crisp "go to it" air of old. He was in touch with many of the Canadian crews we flew with and occasionally sent me snippets of news about them all.

Early in October, 1994, he called me and asked me not to 'phone him for a few weeks as he was going into hospital to have his "starboard kneecap" replaced after which he would be convalescing for a while. If all went well he would then have the "port" one done as well. He assured me that he had just had a full medical check up and "he was 100%". In late November I tried to call him but could get no reply. I finally contacted his son, John, who informed me that Robbie had recovered from the operation but was having a hard time suffering a lot of pain getting up the stairs and had been back to hospital for more therapy.

On 1st December John called me to say Robbie had been found dead in his bed by one of his 'Legion' friends the previous day. Apparently he had had a heart attack. The funeral was to take place the following day, 2nd December, so there was just time to send a wreath to the Skipper from the crew of 'Jug and Bottle'.

A year or so after seeing Mo in 1987 I learnt that his health had started to deteriorate. His eyesight began to fail and he was forced to give up driving. I learnt from his daughter, Sheila, that he had suffered several slight strokes which probably accounted for his occasional grumpiness. By January 1992 he could no longer care for himself adequately and entered a 'Veterans' home but then it was found he had cancer. Recovering, after an apparently successful operation, he fell and fractured his pelvis and died in September, 1993.

A widower for seventeen years, he had lived alone in the house he and his wife had built but he was content to be left in peace and pursue his hobby of 'fixing things' in his workshop. To the end he would have nothing to do with 'those goddam planes'. I'll never have that cup of coffee with him now.

Gibby also is retired after a peace time career in the R.C.A.F. In typical Canadian fashion he thinks nothing of driving hundreds and hundreds of miles from his home in Ottawa to places as far apart as Nova Scotia or Calgary. Last year he and his wife, Joan, made a 14,000 miles motor home tour of Canada and the States. Monty, now a 'bachelor boy' again, is also retired and still, apparently, has an eye for the girls. He travels around Canada quite a lot and seems to keep in touch with former colleagues from coast to coast in the pursuit of his new career as a photographer.

Poker and Annie retired to a little village in Scotland where, as Poker puts it, there is peace. We meet occasionally at Squadron reunions and Paddy and I call when on holiday in the vicinity. Ronnie, of course, is no longer with us but we remember him as on the occasion when Monty gave a little dinner party. The toast was, "Absent friends – Ronnie." If the four of us who are left ever get together again we shall have to add Robbie and Mo – three toasts – separately – Robbie would have liked that.

As for me, the immediate post-war years were not so good. Towards the end of the war the family wool business closed down following the death of my father and his partner. As referred to earlier, a navigator's wing and a tour of ops were no qualifications for a job in 'civvie street' and I eventually 'remustered' into a job in catering. I did, in fact, try to get on a teacher training course but there seemed to be a long delay at the time. Freda died suddenly of 'polio' in the 1949 epidemic and by then we had a three year old son, Ian, who, incidentally, was the driving force behind this story. "Get it all down on paper," said he. 1953 opened a new phase in my life when I married Paddy since when, we have added two daughters and another son to our family which is now augmented by a clutch of grandchildren! After a few more ups and downs which included a short 'tour' of gold mining in Kirkland Lake, Northern Ontario I eventually qualified as a teacher.

I look back on the Squadron days with affection and pride and feel happy to be associated with it again. Seeing Robbie, Poker, Monty, Gibby and Mo again gave me a sense of "rounding things off" or "tidying it all up." Our numbers are declining quickly now. With increasing frequency we hear of a respected comrade who has passed on. For a time there is a feeling of sadness which blends into a sense of nostalgia as we recall his presence amongst us, his spirit, his humour and his philosophy. One such man, Squadron Leader George Pirie, D.F.C., was my Station Navigation Officer who died shortly after a Squadron reunion. His philosophy was: "Every day is a bonus."

STATION BULLETIN.

No. 21.

NOT TO BE TAKEN OFF THE STATION.
31st March, 1945.

SPECIAL EDITION.

MESSAGE FROM STATION COMMANDER.

It is with the greatest regret that I have to confirm the news that is now general knowledge. The Squadron is moving out on Monday, 2nd April and the Station will close down almost immediately afterwards. Although a care and maintenance party will remain, everyone, except personnel of 5015 Artisan Flight should anticipate early posting and prepare themselves accordingly.

The business of packing up affects everyone. Individually, personnel, particularly Inventory holders, should see that they are properly cleared before leaving the Station. Failure to get your clearance chit signed by the Adjutant causes a good deal of trouble and is likely to result in 664B action where anything is missing. Not only should individuals get their personal affairs shipshape and tidy but Squadron Commanders are under an obligation to see that all their quarters are left clean and in good order. There will be a 'marching out' inspection of every building before it is vacated.

Before saying goodbye I should like to thank everyone on the Station for their whole hearted loyalty and support. We are disbanding now because we have done our job, and done it so well that the Hun has been broken sooner than anyone ever dared to hope, even a year ago.

I am well aware that many of you, like myself, leave Grimsby with great regrets but when you go you can justly take pride in the fact that you have made a very real contribution towards the achievements of the Station and thus to win the war.

Where all have done so well it would be invidious to mention any section or person by name but to say goodbye without mentioning the Squadron would be unpardonable.

100 Squadron is a great Squadron because it has the right spirit – a great fighting spirit when on ops and a friendly, co-operative spirit when at home. 100 Squadron has always identified itself with the Station; it has supported the Station in everything; it has encouraged the Station to support it in everything. We are happy to have had 100 as our Squadron and, in saying goodbye , I know I am joined by every member of the Station in wishing it: GOOD LUCK, GOOD BOMBING, AND NO EARLY RETURNS.

To all the others I have been privileged to command during the past year, I confess I am sorry indeed, to have to leave you before the war is won. I thank you again for good work and your co-operation and sincerely hope fortune favours you in the future.

IAN S. NEWBIGGIN.
G|Captain.

APPENDIX 2

CITATIONS

DISTINGUISHED FLYING CROSS

A|S|L David Robb, AFC, (O) CAN (J9545).
100 Sqn. R.A.F.
Trained at 4 I.T.S. 10 EFTS, and
15 SFTS.

"Squadron Leader Robb has participated in a number of operations against major German targets. Throughout he has displayed outstanding leadership both in the air and on the ground which, combined with his exemplary zeal, courage and devotion to duty have been most praiseworthy. In October, 1944, during an attack against Emmerich a fire broke out in his aircraft. Three of the petrol tanks were punctured and some of the instruments were damaged. The fire was extinguished and Squadron Leader Robb pressed home his attack. His skilful airmanship and resourcefulness have won the admiration of his crew."

(Eff. 15th March, 1945)
(Auth: LG 36997)
d|23 Mar|45

AIR FORCE CROSS

Flt. Lt. David Robb CAN (J9545)

"In recognition of distinguished services rendered while engaged on flying duties with the Royal Canadian Air Force overseas.

DISTINGUISHED FLYING CROSS

Flg. Off. Elmer Marshall Mosure, CAN (J37890)
100 Sqn. R.A.F. (now retired)

Trained at 7 ITS, 2 BGS and 5 OAS."Flying Officer Mosure has now completed his first operational tour. During an attack on Emmerich in October, 1944, his aircraft was severely damaged and fire broke out in the nose of the aircraft. This officer fought with the flames until they were subdued and succeeded in preventing a serious situation. Flying Officer Mosure is an officer of cool resource and courage and has at all times shown a high standard of devotion to duty." (Eff. 8th September, 1945.)

SQUADRON SONGS

THE HUNDRED SQUADRON BOYS

(To MacNamara's Band)

Oh we are 100 Squadron we're the boys who know the score,
If anyone denies it we will spread them on the floor;
At bombing and beer and billiards and all the Cleethorpes hops
We've got the gen we're the leading men,
We certainly are the tops!

CHORUS
Whilst the bombs go bang and flak bursts clang and the
searchlights blaze away
We weave all over the starry sky and wish we'd gone by day,
Oh Hamilton, Hamilton, save us now we can't abide the noise,
A credit to Butch Harris are the 100 Squadron boys!

We love to nip off smartly to a little buzz bomb site
And smartly nip off home again and get to bed at night;
We're saving our night vision up for other earthly joys
And now we're safely in the Mess meet 100 Squadron boys.

    CHORUS

I'm Wing Commander Hamilton and I am Number One

I very strongly deprecate the things that are not done;
If you ask my crew if I have any faults they'll tell you in accents sweet:
You can see the ants as we stooge over France at altitude zero feet.

CHORUS

My name's Dave Robb and they gave me the job of settling
A Flight's hash,
Three ops a year and gallons of beer and look at the extra cash;
Believe it or not this ribbon I've got, diagonal white and red
Was won for drinking fifteen pints in fifteen seconds dead!

CHORUS

My name is Scott and I'm rather hot at dishing out the bull;
I don't believe in wrapping my Flight in yards of cotton wool.
Flannel's the stuff if you flannel enough but you can't flannel me
So that'll be five bob in the box and a couple of hours P.T.

CHORUS

My name is Traff and I joined the RAF, well very near the start,
My trade is navigation though I'm a bit of a wolf at heart,
I've a popsy here and a popsy there and I don't care if they're wed
So long as their husbands don't come home and find me still in bed.

CHORUS

I get my beer from the bombardiers my name is Zaggerman,
So raise your hat to a desert rat, the Laurence of El San;
I lost my curls to the harem girls who thought me lots of fun

For I was never known to overshoot or make a dummy run!

CHORUS

I'm Flight Lieutenant Thompson once the terror of Tobruk
My desert dicing days would fill a pretty weighty book,
But since I got to Grimsby they've demoted me By Heck!
And now I'm one of the lesser shieks of Barnetby le Beck.

CHORUS

My Name's O'Donovan Iland and I'm Number One A.G.
And 109s and 190s don't mean a thing to me;
I'll man the mid-upper with any old skipper, so long as he's
learned to fly
You can only live once, it's a matter of months, and it doesn't
take long to die.

CHORUS

My name is Waite and I'm sorry I'm late my train has just
got in,
I've just got back from Scunthorpe where I'm living in part
time sin;
There's a girl named Sue, she'd appeal to you – if you haven't
been introduced
She's big and blonde and terribly fond of me and my plus 12
boost!
CHORUS

(Flt. Lt. Lampitt.)

BEHIND THOSE SWINGING DOORS

'Twas Saturday night and the ops room was chill
Though the "King's Head" was merry and gay
And Groupie and Wingco and Bradford did wait
For the Form B that was on its way.
"What's keeping those aircrew?" the Wingco exclaimed,
"They ought to be up here," he said,
And little they knew, that every darned crew
Was safely inside the "King's Head!

CHORUS
Oh the doors swing in . . . the doors swing out
The aircrew pass in but they seldom pass out.
The Squadron I fear has gone right on the beer
Behind those swinging doors . . . Behind those swinging doors.

"I've tannoyed and tannoyed," the S.I.O. moaned,
"But no-one has answered my call;
The ops meals are spoiled and the cooks are all oiled
In the Flights there is no-one at all!"
Dear Squadron, Dear Squadron come back to us now
There's briefing at quarter to three
The Wingco is groaning with tears in his eyes,
'Oh bring back my Squadron to me.' "

CHORUS

Oh the doors swing in . . .. the doors swing out
The aircrew pass in but they seldom pass out
You can stuff all your ops whilst there's plenty of hops
Behind those swinging doors . . . . .Behind those swinging doors
At last Groupie guessed at the horrible truth
And down to the village they went ;
They drove with a roar right up to the door
And called on the boys to repent.

"Dear Squadron," they wailed, "In your duty you've failed
You'd better start mending your ways
In time to save Groupie from losing a ring
It's always the C.O. who pays!"

CHORUS

Oh the doors swing in, the doors swing out,
The aircrew all heard them but never came out.
They said, "It's our right to drink Saturday night
Behind those swinging doors . . . Behind those swinging doors."
Each Saturday night at the "King's Head" Saloon
The Squadron blows in with its pay
And they spend it on beers till it's up to their ears
And never go home till it's day!
"Dear Squadron," Butch Harris wrote after a while,
"I've heard of your Saturday night.
If you press on regardless the other six days
You can take it from me . . . It's alright!"

CHORUS

Oh the doors swing in, the doors swing out,
The aircrew pass in but they seldom pass out
And Butch is there too, just imbibing a few
Behind those swinging doors . . . Behind those swinging doors!

OPS IN AN OXFORD

AIR: WIDDICOMBE FAIR.

Bill Pope, Bill Pope, come lend us a kite,
All along, out along, down along lee,
For we want to go to the Ruhr tonight
With George Pirie, Jack Hamblin, Tommy Thompson, Frank Fox
Eric Haddingham, Vin Knight and old Uncle Newbiggin and All
And Uncle Newbiggin and All.

We are a sprog crew but we must see it through,
All along, out along, down along lee,
If we haven't got a Lanc, well an Oxford will do
With George Pirie..etc.

So Bill Pope he filled up the Oxford with gas
A fifty pound bomb and a sleeping out pass.

The old Oxford groaned when the crew climbed aboard,
We levered them in with a stout piece of board.

How that poor kite took off is a mystery yet
And five hundred feet was the highest she'd get.

George Pirie he found he'd no room for his chart
But that didn't matter – he knew it by heart.

When they reached the Dutch coast Groupy started to weave
And half of the crew begged permission to leave.

They flew into cloud – there was icing and frost
And after an hour they were hopelessly lost.

They suddenly saw, far ABOVE them a town
The Skipper said:"Well now, we're right upside down."

208

Jack Hamblin was nursing his fifty pound bomb
Till his hands and his feet and his knees had gone numb.

And when they inverted, as if to give proof
It slipped from his grasp and went crash through the roof.

"Bomb Gone!" said Jack Hamblin. The rest said, "We know!
The question is *where* did the ruddy thing go?"

"Down there," said the Skipper, and there, sure enough,
Bang in the town was a bang and a puff.

The camera turned and recorded the burst
The Skipper said, "Seems boys, we got in there first."

They set course for base – or where George said it was
When they asked how he knew he replied, "Just because."

And seven days later they sighted Spurn Head
Then acres of fog and the aerodrome Red.

They landed her blind and downwind with a bump
And the people in Holton le Clay felt the thump.

When the cheering had died and the lines were all shot
The S.I.O. started the photos to plot.

Then he leaped from his chair and exclaimed, "Well I'm hanged!
It wasn't the Ruhr – it was Binbrook you pranged!"

(Flt. Lt. Lampitt.)

ACKNOWLEDGEMENTS

TO: GOFF
For your friendship. For the South African days and for starting it all off.

TO SQUADRON LEADER DAVE ROBB, DFC, AFC.
For never overshooting. For a lot of happy landings. For the odd 'cover up'. For being Robbie!

TO: FLYING OFFICER ELMER MOSURE, DFC.
For putting out that fire! For all your aiming points. For many a fatherly word of advice!

TO: FLIGHT SERGEANT ARTHUR GAMBLE.
For passing Mo the fire extinguishers! For many a laugh. For getting 1.1 m.p.g. out of a Lanc and for keeping Robbie awake with the coffee! And particularly for your help in getting this together.

TO: FLIGHT SERGEANT RONNIE BROWN.
For those Q.D.M.s! For getting all the latest gen on the Squadron. For helping me with those astro shots and the song writing!

TO: PILOT OFFICER R.G. GIBSON.
For looking after the back end of the kite and those awful corkscrews!

TO: PILOT OFFICER C.M. KERR.
For having a crack at that jet and helping Gibby with the corkscrews! To both of you for being the eyes of the crew.

TO: URSULA MOESSNER.
For giving me a deeper insight into the Pforzheim raid.

TO: AUDREY GREALY.
For your poetry which brought it all back.

TO: MARTIN MIDDLEBROOK & CHRIS EVERITT.
(BOMBER COMMAND WAR DIARIES -VIKING.)
For enabling me to fill in some of the gaps.

TO: GROUP CAPTAIN DUDLEY SAWARD. "BOMBER HARRIS". (CASSELL).
For the statistics and the narrative which finally damns the critics of Bomber Command.

TO: FRANCIS K. MASON. "THE AVRO LANCASTER" (ASTON).
For finding out what happened to all those lovely Lancs!

TO MARY WILKINSON (SQUARE ONE PUBLICATIONS)
For your advice and encouragement in getting this book into print.